For Rylan and Ashton.
—Gareth Long

For Rachel and Florence.
—Harvey Grout

For Rach and family.
—Stuart Taylor

CONTENTS

Preface   viii

GAMES

PREFACE

We'll try not to keep you reading this too long since the best part of this book is the games. However, before you try them out, we will briefly explain why we believe that interactive games can be a great strategy for enhancing motivation and learning within the classroom, and why this should be a book that you keep in your classroom, ready to use!

Although they have many benefits, the best is their use in the classroom to help your pupils review what they already know about a subject or topic; games can help them relate the topic to enjoyable learning experiences and important study skills; and finally, games can be used prior to formal and informal assessments. Traditionally, teachers have too often provided pupils with information, and then assessed whether it has been remembered through a show of hands or tests and exams. We feel that games offer an additional way of contributing to a stimulating learning environment and provide an additional method for assessing learning. In short, we feel that the use of games can make learning more memorable, fun, and successful.

Interactive games are those in which there may be interaction with the environment, interaction with other pupils, interaction with tasks and problems, and of course, interaction with the teacher. If there can also be movement, music, and friendly competition, it's even better!

The games in this book can be used in a variety of ways. They are designed to be used as an effective starter activity, for the middle part of a lesson to reignite learning at a time when pupils may potentially switch off, or as a final plenary activity to assess pupil learning. Furthermore, they may be recommended to pupils and parents for learning outside the school environment. The games are arranged alphabetically, but we've included the key benefits at the top of each game so that you can see them at a glance while flipping through the book.

We hope that you like the 101 interactive classroom games outlined in this book; we hope even more that you play them with your class; and most of all, we hope that you adapt and improve them! All we ask is that if you do make changes, please let us know by contacting us at info@sport-iq.com.

GAMES

Ace of Spades

Promote discussion about possible answers.
Work in groups.

Equipment

- A pack of cards
- A set of questions

Description

A pack of cards (with numbers 2 to 10) is spread out face down on a table at the back of the class, and the pupils stand at the front of the class.

The teacher reads a question (or it is projected onto the white-board), and without any talking, the pupils move to the cards; each turns over one card. The pupils then move to the table that corresponds with their number card (for instance, all pupils who turn over a four meet at table four).

The pupils discuss the question with their teammates, and after a set period of time, provide an answer. If the answer is correct, all team members get 10 points. The class then returns the cards to the original table and returns to the front of the class for the next question. Pupils will form a new team for each question. Pupils keep their own scores to see how many points they get by the end of the lesson.

Variations

Easier: Put the ace of spades in the pack. If a pupil picks that card, she can join a table of her choice, and if that table gets the question right, each pupil scores double points.

Harder: Have an uneven number of cards on the table (for instance, only two 5s). Therefore, some teams will have fewer pupils than others to discuss the answer.

All Bases Covered

Learn key concepts and definitions.
Practice multiple-choice questions and answers.

Equipment

- One A B C D card for each pupil (see page 4)
- 10 markers per pupil (counters or poker chips work well)
- Prepared multiple-choice questions

Description

This game is based on the TV game show Dual. Provide each pupil with a card that has an A, B, C and D on it. Each pupil will also need 10 markers.

Read or display a multiple-choice question, and have each pupil choose the correct answer by covering it with a marker. Reveal the right answer, and instruct the pupils that they may keep any marker covering a correct answer; any markers that are placed on incorrect answers are returned to the teacher. A pupil is out of the game if he fails to cover the correct answer with a marker (he may then join a classmate).

If the pupil is convinced he knows the answer, he will only use one marker (on the correct answer) and therefore will still have 10 markers at the end of the question. If he has no idea of the answer, he may use a marker on each answer (this way he will stay in the game but lose 3 markers).

You might play until only one pupil is left or to a set period of time and see which pupil has the most markers remaining.

Variations

Easier: Allow the pupils one lifeline that allows them to get out of their seats and look at their classmates' answers.

Harder: Give pupils a different number of markers when starting the game.

Cards for All Bases Covered

From G. Long, H. Grout, and S. Taylor, 2011, *101 Classroom Games* (Champaign, IL: Human Kinetics).

Amnesia

Learn how to ask questions.
Practice recall and interpretation.

Equipment

- Post-it notes
- Pens

Description

Place your pupils in groups of five or six and have them sit in a circle facing each other. Give the pupils a category from the subject area being studied and ask them to write down a concept or keyword on a Post-it without anyone else seeing it. Pupils place the completed Post-it on the forehead of the person to their left.

Taking it in turns, each pupil is allowed to ask a question of each of the other players within the circle in order to find out what is written on their own note. The other players can only answer yes or no to the questions. Pupils should keep track of the number of questions they must ask before they can determine the content of the Post-it. The pupil who asks the fewest questions wins.

Variations

Easier: Make the subject areas simple to guess by limiting the number of keywords available.

Harder: Place a time limit on the question period for each pupil.

4

Baseball

Learn key concepts.
Practice answering questions under pressure.
Provide more than one answer.

Equipment

A set of questions

Description

Pupils play this game in teams of three. Half of the teams consist of a pitcher and two fielders. The other half each has three batters. The batting teams play against the pitching teams.

To play, the first pupil on the batting team steps up to the plate. The pitcher on the opposing team fires a question (which must have at least 4 possible answers) at the batsman who has 20 seconds to answer. If she gives one correct answer, she moves to first base; two correct answers get her to second base; three correct answers move her to third base; and four correct answers are a home run.

However, if the batsman doesn't provide all four answers, then the two fielders have the opportunity to answer. If they can provide one more correct answer to the question, then the batsman is out. Each incorrect answer (including no answer) is a strike. Three strikes and the batsman is out.

Once the batters' team is all out, the fielding team goes to bat. The team that scores the most runs wins.

Variations

Easier: Play in larger teams or allow the team of three to collaborate on an answer.

Harder: Allow only 10-15 seconds for pupils to answer.

Basketball

Learn key concepts and definitions.
Use textbooks to locate answers.

Equipment

- Basketball board (see page 8)
- Die
- A set of questions

Description

The aim of the game is to score as many points as possible. Pupils play against each other in groups or pairs. The first player rolls the die and moves the number of squares shown on the die. What the pupil does next depends on the square he lands on.

Question	He answers a question.
Pass	He answers a question, but he is able to use his text-book.
Dribble	He rolls the dice again.
Foul	His turn is over, and the next pupil rolls the die.
Shoot	If he answers the question correctly, he scores a 3-point basket and starts back at the beginning.
Layup	If he answers the question correctly, he scores a 2-point basket and starts back at the beginning.

If a pupil answers a question incorrectly, or if he lands on a foul square, his turn is over and it is the next pupil's turn. The aim is to score as many points as possible in the time the match is taking place.

Variations

Easier: Add more pass squares to the board or work in pairs.

Harder: Before the game begins, the pupils design their own questions, with answers, to ask their partners.

Basketball Board

START	1 QUESTION	2 PASS	3 QUESTION
4 QUESTION	5 DRIBBLE	6 QUESTION	7 QUESTION
8 DRIBBLE	9 FOUL	10 QUESTION	11 PASS
12 QUESTION	13 QUESTION	14 SHOOT	15 FOUL
16 DRIBBLE	17 QUESTION	18 PASS	19 SHOOT
20 FOUL	21 SHOOT	22 QUESTION	23 FOUL
24 PASS	25 QUESTION	26 DRIBBLE	27 QUESTION
28 QUESTION	29 SHOOT	30 QUESTION	31 SHOOT
32 QUESTION	33 FOUL	34 QUESTION	35 QUESTION
36 SHOOT	37 FOUL	38 LAYUP SHOT	39 QUESTION
40 QUESTION	41 SHOOT	42 SHOOT	43 QUESTION
44 QUESTION	45 LAYUP SHOT	46 FOUL	BASKET SCORED

From G. Long, H. Grout, and S. Taylor, 2011, *101 Classroom Games* (Champaign, IL: Human Kinetics).

Beach Volleyball

Assess knowledge and understanding.
Prepare for examinations.
Use textbooks to locate information.

Equipment

- A set of serve cards (see following examples)
- A textbook

Description

The teacher or pupils prepare a series of serve cards that have questions worth three marks (such as the ones that follow).

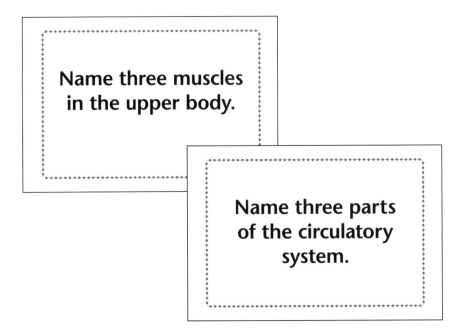

> **Name three muscles in the upper body.**

> **Name three parts of the circulatory system.**

The class is put in teams of two, and one team plays against another (as in beach volleyball). Team A serves and turns over a card for team B to receive.

To score a point, team B has to provide three answers to a question. If they can't provide three answers, then the point goes to team A. In volleyball a player cannot touch the ball twice, so in this game, a team member cannot provide two answers in a row. Both members of the team have to contribute to win a point. Team B then serves and turns over a card for team A. A textbook acts as the referee!

Variations

Easier: Allow the teams a set number of time-outs. When a team decides to use a time-out, they have 45 seconds to find the answer in their books.

Harder: Introduce a set number of blocks that each team can play. In this variation, if team A get three correct answers to a question, team B can play a block, meaning team A has to provide one more example to get the point.

Bidding for Success

Learn key concepts.
Learn facts.

Equipment

Fake money

Description

The goal of this game is to win as many correct statements as possible. Each player/team starts with £100. Begin by reading a statement, which may or may not be true (this will work best if the statements are not easy). Once a statement is read, all players or teams submit a secret bid on paper labeled with their names (see page 12) and hand it to the teacher (like on eBay). If the player or team believes the statement is false, they will put a bid of £0. If they believe it is correct, they will bid a price and hope that they get to buy the statement, whilst not spending all their money. The team with the highest bid wins the statement.

When all statements have been bought, the teacher will indicate whether the statements were true or false. The player or team with the most correct statements is the winner. In the case of a draw, the team who has the most money left is the winner.

Sample Statements

'The pulmonary artery takes blood from the heart to the lungs.' Since this is a true statement, hopefully everyone will bid more than £0. The highest bidder wins the statement and subtracts the money paid from her total.

'The hamstring is made up of four muscles.' Since this is a false statement, hopefully everyone will bid £0. If so, the statement is not purchased. If money is bid, then the highest bidder wins the statement but will find out at the end of the game that her money was wasted!

Variations

Easier: Allow pupils to use a textbook or the Internet for a set time for each question.

Harder: Pupils or teams go bankrupt if they buy a false statement.

Bidding for Success Bids

Name: _____

We would like to bid the following amount of money _____

For statement number_____

- -

Name: _____

We would like to bid the following amount of money _____

For statement number_____

- -

Name: _____

We would like to bid the following amount of money _____

For statement number_____

- -

Name: _____

We would like to bid the following amount of money _____

For statement number_____

- -

Name: _____

We would like to bid the following amount of money _____

For statement number_____

- -

Name: _____

We would like to bid the following amount of money _____

For statement number_____

From G. Long, H. Grout, and S. Taylor, 2011, *101 Classroom Games* (Champaign, IL: Human Kinetics).

Boxing Clever

Learn key concepts and definitions.

Equipment

- A set of boxing cards (see page 14)
- A set of definition cards
- A stopwatch

Description

Pair up the class (so pupil A gets ready to box pupil B). The boxing cards (see page 14) are shuffled and placed in the middle of the pair. Both pupils have a series of definition cards (see the sample definition card; a glossary is a great source for making the definition cards).

Pupil A reads the definition on her first card (see sample). If pupil B guesses what is being described, she gets to turn over one of the boxing cards (see page 14). If she turns over a jab card, she gets 1 point; if she turns over a hook card, she gets 2 points; and if she turns over an uppercut card, she gets 3 points.

> **Definition: Injecting blood that has been removed from the body a few days earlier, enabling the blood to carry more oxygen. It is banned because it's a form of cheating. It can cause kidney and heart failure.**
> **Word: Blood doping**

If a pupil answers incorrectly or takes over 10 seconds to provide an answer, it is pupil A's turn to answer. Each round lasts three minutes, and the pupil with the most points wins the bout. After the three minutes are up, the pupils move on to box another classmate.

Variations

Easier: Allow pupils two attempts at each card or allow them a certain number of blocks that allow them to pass.

Harder: Ask pupils to provide the definition to the word. If the pupil gets the definition word perfect, she scores a knockout and wins straight away.

Boxing Clever Cards

Jab 1 Point	Hook 2 Points	Uppercut 3 Points
Jab 1 Point	Hook 2 Points	Uppercut 3 Points
Jab 1 Point	Hook 2 Points	Uppercut 3 Points
Jab 1 Point	Hook 2 Points	Uppercut 3 Points
Jab 1 Point	Hook 2 Points	Uppercut 3 Points

From G. Long, H. Grout, and S. Taylor, 2011, *101 Classroom Games* (Champaign, IL: Human Kinetics).

Bull's-Eye

Learn key concepts and definitions.

Equipment

- 20 PowerPoint slides (or something similar) of questions
- A dartboard
- 1 dart

Description

Prepare 20 slides or cards with one question on each (you might decide to have a bull's-eye slide as well). Slide 1 has the hardest question whilst slide 20 has the easiest. Split the class into two teams.

One member of the first team throws a dart at a dart board (Velcro darts are good for this game), and the team has to answer the question on the slide that corresponds to the number hit by the dart. Award a set number of points for a correct answer, and then the other team throws a dart. Continue until there are no questions left to answer. The team with the highest marks wins.

Variations

Easier: Have three questions on each slide, and allow the pupils to select the one they answer.

Harder: Have a more difficult question on each slide that is worth double points.

Chain Gangs

Prepare essay arguments or long-answer exam questions.
Share good ideas.

Equipment

- A set of exam questions or essay titles
- A watch, a clock, or an egg timer

Description

The goal of this game is for each team to score as many points as they can. The team scores 1 point for every good thing they say! (Points are awarded by the teacher.)

The teams line up like a chain, and the teacher asks an open question such as 'Why is exercise important for a healthy lifestyle?' and starts the clock (for instance, for one minute).

The first pupil in the chain begins to answer the question, trying to score as many points as possible. When he runs out of things to say, he passes, and the next pupil in the line takes over.

You should have one sound to use to indicate something good or accurate has been said (such as striking a percussion triangle), and another sound that indicates something not very good (for instance, blowing a party noisemaker). After the time is up, the next chain gang steps forward for their question and tries to get the highest score.

Variations

Easier: Allow the pupils to decide on the order of their chain.

Harder: Add the rule that all the members of the chain must have scored at least 1 point before the time runs out (in other words, everyone must speak); otherwise the team scores 0!

Championship Golf

Learn key concepts.
Answer fact-based questions.

Equipment

- A golf scorecard (see page 18)
- A piece of A4 paper for each pupil
- 18 questions

Description

The class will play a round of golf. The teacher will ask the class 18 questions, one at a time, and set a time limit for writing the answer. Each question is a hole, and par for each hole equals the number of answers the pupils need to provide. For example, if hole 1 is a par 4, the question could be 'Name four methods of training.'

How to Score

For each hole, the teacher asks a question, and the pupils write their answers on their papers. If par for the hole is 4, and the pupil writes 4 correct answers, she has made par and her score is 0.

If the pupil provides an additional answer, then she gets a birdie. For instance, if she names five methods of training, her score would be –1, a birdie. And if on the first hole, a pupil names seven methods of training, she would score –3, a hole-in-one. Remember in golf a low score is good!

However, if she were only able to name 3 methods of training, the pupil would have scored a bogey and get a score of +1. Once all pupils in the class have completed the hole (written their answers on their papers), the teacher will read out the correct answers. The class champion is the person who shoots the lowest round.

Variations

Easier: Allow some people to work in pairs; the caddy can have access to the textbook or the Internet and help the golfer with the answer.

Harder: Decrease the set time allowed for answering a question, or increase the par score from 70 to 80 so more answers are required.

Championship Golf Scorecard

Hole	Par	Score
1	4	
2	3	
3	4	
4	4	
5	4	
6	4	
7	4	
8	3	
9	5	
10	4	
11	3	
12	5	
13	4	
14	3	
15	4	
16	3	
17	4	
18	5	
Score	70	

From G. Long, H. Grout, and S. Taylor, 2011, *101 Classroom Games* (Champaign, IL: Human Kinetics).

Connect 4

Learn a topic in depth.

Equipment

- Connect 4 boards or draw a 7 × 7 grid on paper (see page 20)
- A set of questions

Description

Pupils compete against each other in a game of Connect 4. Each individual game has a different problem for pupils to solve, such as naming the bones in the human body. Pupils rotate going first.

Pupil A will offer one answer to the question (in this case, fibula); if he is correct, he can place a piece in the board (or mark his place on the grid). Pupil B will then attempt to provide another answer to the same question (for instance, femur), and if correct, can place a piece in the board. If an answer is incorrect, the pupil may not place a piece in the board, and the next pupil has his go. The game continues until either pupil has four pieces in a horizontal or diagonal row.

If neither pupil is able to answer correctly, and neither has connected four, then the game is declared null, and the pupils must spend 10 minutes researching the answers before playing the same game again.

Variations

Easier: Provide the class with the questions at the start of the lesson and give them suitable time to consider their responses.

Harder: Pupils must provide two answers for each question; for instance, fibula and femur.

Connect 4 Board

Player 1 = X, Player 2 = O

From G. Long, H. Grout, and S. Taylor, 2011, *101 Classroom Games* (Champaign, IL: Human Kinetics).

Crossfire

Learn key concepts.
Think quickly under pressure.

Equipment

A set of questions

Description

The pupils stand in a circle with the teacher in the middle of the circle. The teacher points to two pupils in the circle and asks a quick question. Once either pupil knows the answer to the question, she points to her opponent and then answers the question.

If the answer is correct, the pupil beats her opponent, who is then out of the competition (the eliminated pupil sits down in the circle). If the answer is incorrect, the pupil has fired a blank, and her opponent has an opportunity to fire back with the correct answer. If neither pupil is correct, both remain in the game, but each must raise one finger to indicate a loss of one life. If a pupil loses three lives, she is eliminated from the game and sits down in the circle. The last pupil standing in the circle is the winner.

Variations

Easier: Speed up the game by using multiple-choice questions; the pupils then only have to choose the answer they think is correct.

Harder: Pupils are eliminated if they answer incorrectly or if they are unable to provide an answer.

Definition Bingo

Learn key concepts and definitions.

Equipment

- A bingo card for each pupil
- A list of keywords numbered 1 through 16 for each pupil
- A glossary for the keywords

Description

Pupils place the numbers 1 through 16 randomly in the 16 boxes on their bingo card (so all pupils should now have different bingo cards). The teacher, or one of the pupils (who can use a glossary), reads out the definition to one of the 16 keywords. When a pupil thinks the quizmaster is describing a particular keyword, he crosses off the relevant number on his card. Once a pupil has a line of four numbers crossed off, he shouts, 'Winner!' The pupil then recites the numbers he crossed off, and if these have been read out, he is declared the winner.

Example: Keywords for the circulatory system

1. Aorta	9. White blood cells
2. Vena cava	10. Platelets
3. Pulmonary vein	11. Haemoglobin
4. Pulmonary artery	12. Veins
5. Ventricle	13. Arteries
6. Atrium	14. Capillaries
7. Plasma	15. Deoxygenated
8. Red blood cells	16. Oxygenated

Variations

Easier: Allow the pupils to play definition bingo in pairs or groups.

Harder: Add another nine words and play again, using a 5 x 5 table.

Harder: Reverse the game so that you have the definitions numbered, and when the quizmaster reads out a keyword, pupils have to match the correct definition.

Domes and Dishes

Show an extended range of knowledge.
Practice short-answer examination questions.

Equipment

- 20 cones (or coins)
- A set of three-part questions

Description

You may play this game either as a 1v1 game or as a team game (domes versus dishes), with a quizmaster who has a set of questions (each with 3 or more answers). Set out 20 cones on a table or the floor. Ten cones should be placed as normal (domes), and the other 10 cones are turned upside down (dishes). Begin by asking the Domes a question. They must try to provide one or more correct answers. For each correct answer, the team changes a dish to a dome. After their turn has finished, the next question is directed to the Dishes. For each correct response, the Dishes turn a dome into a dish. At the end of the questions, the team that has converted the most cones into their own form wins.

Variations

Easier: Give the pupils one minute to get the three correct answers.

Harder: If an answer is incorrect, then the team must turn over one of their own cones.

Faster, Higher, Stronger

Learn key concepts.
Write longer examination answers.

Equipment

- A set of faster, higher, stronger, and boycott cards for each pupil (see page 25)
- A set of questions

Description

Each pupil has four cards: a faster card, a higher card, a stronger card, and a boycott card. The teacher puts an exam question on the board or projector screen like the following one.

Read this to the pupils: 'Many major sporting events take place throughout the world. These have often been affected by political or financial issues. Give two examples of such events. For each example identified, describe the political or financial issue involved and describe what happened (worth six marks).'

Give the pupils a set time (perhaps three minutes) to write an answer to the question. Pupils score points as they would in an exam, so pupils whose answers are fully correct will earn the full six marks. However, if a pupil is confident that she will get full marks on the question, she can get extra marks by playing one of her cards. If she plays her faster card, she must finish writing before the three minutes are up (one extra mark plus full marks for the correct answer). If she plays her higher card, she can score one extra mark for every mark earned for the correct answer.

If she plays her stronger card, the teacher will give her a harder question. So in the previous example, the question may be reworded to 'Give two examples from the 1980s.' Each correct answer is worth double points. It is the responsibility of the pupil to keep count of their own score. If she is not confident, she can play her boycott card and spend the time reading about that topic in her book.

Variations

Easier: Increase the amount of times a pupil can use the boycott card.

Harder: Insist that half the group play one of the faster, higher, or stronger cards for each question.

Faster, Higher, Stronger Cards

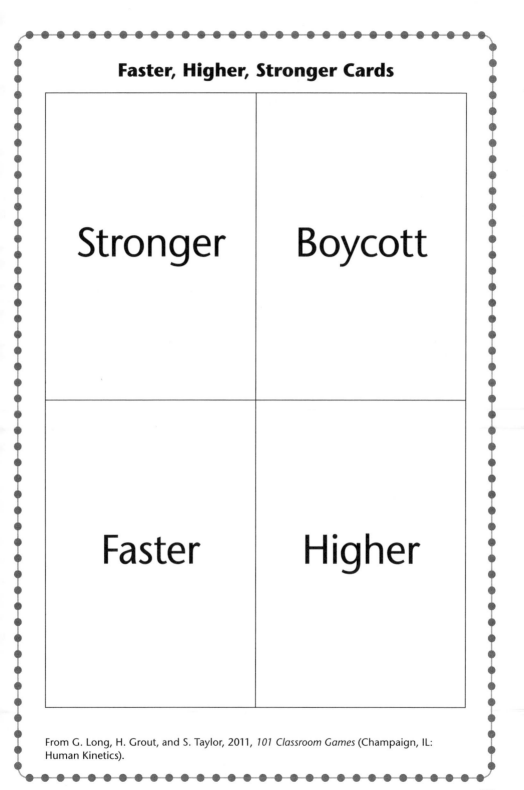

Stronger	Boycott
Faster	Higher

From G. Long, H. Grout, and S. Taylor, 2011, *101 Classroom Games* (Champaign, IL: Human Kinetics).

Fortune Teller

Design questions.
Work with many different pupils.

Equipment

- An A4 piece of paper for each pupil
- Fortune teller instructions (see pages 27-29)

Description

This game is adapted from the classic children's paper-folding game called Fortune Teller (you will find this on the Internet if you have not played it as a child). Each pupil will make her own fortune teller (see pages 27-29). The difference here is that instead of revealing one's fortune (e.g., 'you will be rich!'), it will reveal a question that another pupil will have to answer.

Once the pupils have made their fortune tellers, they walk around the classroom, meet another pupil, and have one go at each other's fortune teller before moving on. You may ask them to keep score of how many questions they answer correctly.

Variations

Easier: Allow the pupils to provide one clue for each of their questions.

Harder: Permit the pupils to ask one of their questions only if they get their opponent's question correct.

Fortune Teller

1. Using an A4 piece of paper fold the short edge diagonally to make a square and tear off the remaining paper.

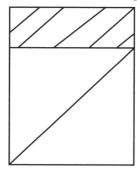

2. Now fold across the other diagonal so you have a folded cross in your square.

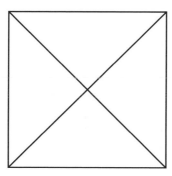

3. Fold each corner to the centre of the square.

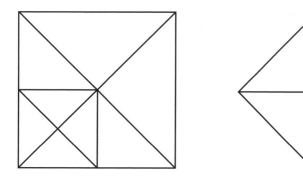

From G. Long, H. Grout, and S. Taylor, 2011, *101 Classroom Games* (Champaign, IL: Human Kinetics).

4. Turn it over and repeat by folding each corner in to the centre of the square.

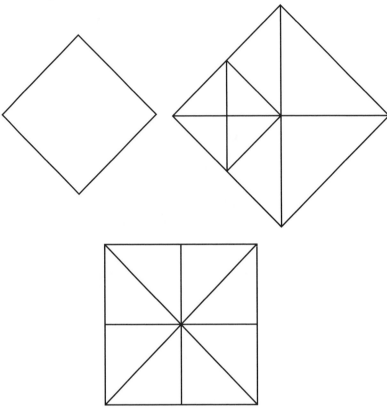

5. Now fold in half and unfold again and turn paper a quarter turn and fold in half and unfold. Now slide your finger and thumb underneath the paper at the back on both sides. Move your fingers and thumbs together to open up different sides of the game.

From G. Long, H. Grout, and S. Taylor, 2011, *101 Classroom Games* (Champaign, IL: Human Kinetics).

6. Label the four visible sides with four words with a different number of letters (e.g., Yellow, Blue, Red, and Green).

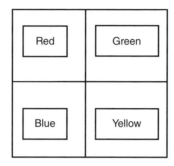

7. On the inside number each segment 1 to 8.

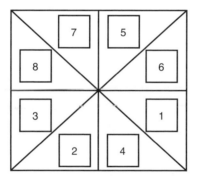

8. Underneath each number you need to write an exam question of your choice. You need to know and retain the answer for each question either on a separate piece of paper or in your head.

9. To play the game, the person playing chooses a colour. If they choose red, the game is moved three times (opened vertically, opened horizontally, opened vertically). Then they select a number (e.g., 6) and the game is moved six times; they then select another number and the flap is lifted and the question is asked.

From G. Long, H. Grout, and S. Taylor, 2011, *101 Classroom Games* (Champaign, IL: Human Kinetics).

Four in a Row

Learn key concepts and definitions.
Develop strategizing and cognitive processes.
Reinforce understanding of material.

Equipment

- Coloured bibs for each team
- Hoops

Description

This simple class game can be used for a lesson starter or a quick-fire test. Place the hoops or markers on the classroom floor in a 6 × 6 grid.

Separate the class into either two or four teams, each indicated by a colour, and place them on the outside of the playing area. Give each team their respective coloured bibs or paper markers. Select a starter question from a random topic and open it up to all teams to answer. The first team with the correct answer is then given the first question on a specific topic.

If a team answers correctly, they get to send a player into the playing grid. Encourage some tactical thinking here from your pupils, both in terms of placement and in terms of who they send from their team (for instance, if one member of the team perceives this topic as a weakness, send him in first). If a team answers incorrectly, the same question is passed clockwise to the next team and continues to do so until the question has been answered correctly. Once the teacher has awarded a correct answer a new question is asked. The winning team is the first team to create a line of four team members, making four in a row.

Variations

Easier: Make the playing grid larger to allow for breakaway lines of four to be started so that teams have to use strategy and tactics in order to block other teams.

Harder: Bring in new rules such as restricting entry to the grid to the player who answered correctly.

Full House

Work on keyword recognition.
Practice working under pressure.

Equipment

PowerPoint or similar presentation software, projector, and screen, or flipchart and pens

Description

Before the lesson, decide on a broad topic that you intend to review (for example, the human body). Within that wider topic, compose questions that can have multiple answers (for instance, 'What are the components of the respiratory system?'). Once you have decided this, select the five most common answers (keywords) and place them in rank order from most commonly thought of to the least commonly thought of. For this example, you may rank lungs as the most common answer. Place the question and the combination of possible answers on two pages of your chosen method of presentation.

Divide the class into two teams. Elect a player from each team to stand at the front of the class. Once the first question is revealed, the elected players should raise a hand to answer. The first to raise his hand can offer a keyword. If the keyword is in the top five, he can decide, with his team, to name all five keywords—a full house—or he can pass, and his opponents must attempt to do the same. If the team names two consecutive keywords that are not on the list, the challenge goes to the other team for completion and a chance to steal that round.

After each round, reveal the answers to the question and then elect two new players to answer a new question and continue the game.

Variations

Easier: Reduce or increase the number of attempts you give to the responding team.

Harder: Make a longer rank-ordered list (perhaps 10 keywords) for the pupils to identify.

Good Arrows

Learn definitions and key concepts.
Recognise how questions are directed in examinations.

Equipment

- Dartboard
- Three darts
- A set of questions

Description

The goal of the game is to score 301 as quickly as possible. Pupils work in pairs and decide who the dart thrower is and who will answer the questions. The first dart thrower has three shots at the dartboard to score as many points as possible. The difficulty of the question asked is determined by the number of points the thrown darts earn. If the points are

0 to 29	easy question
30 to 59	medium question
60 and over	hard question

After each three darts, the points are calculated, and the appropriate question is asked. The team earns the points scored by the darts only if they answer the question correctly. If the pupil answering the question is unable to provide an answer, then her partner can answer the question, but the score is halved. After three rounds, the pupils swap over roles. The first pair to score 301 or more wins.

Variations

Easier: Reduce the distance the darts are thrown. All darts that land in the red areas are worth double points.

Harder: Pupils must finish on exactly 301 to win the game. Pupils must finish on a double.

Great Balls of Fire!

Learn key concepts and definitions.
Practice multiple-choice questions.
Improve recall and response.

Equipment

- Four buckets
- Four different-coloured balls
- Multiple-choice questions

Description

Select five teams and give each team their own coloured balls (you could also use bibs or cones). Label four buckets A, B, C, and D, and line them up in front of the teams.

Read (or project) a multiple-choice question with four possible answers (A, B, C, and D) to all the teams. As soon as the person at the front of his queue thinks he knows the correct answer, he runs and drops his ball in the bucket matching the answer's letter. Teams earn 10 points for the correct answer. A bonus of 10 points is awarded to the team who first answers correctly.

Variations

Easier: Each team could also be given a ball of fire which, when used, doubles their points; if they use their ball of fire, get the correct answer, and do it first, they get 40 points.

Harder: The teacher may include a five-second gamble period before the balls are locked in the bucket. This would allow teams to fake the answer to confuse the other teams.

Hand Over Hand

Learn key concepts and definitions.
Work on short-answer questions.
Improve recall and response time.

Equipment

Bibs of different colours

Description

Split the class into teams and give each team bibs of one colour. Send one member of each team to a group (so each group should have one person from each colour). Once in the group, they all put one of their hands in the circle on top of each other.

The teacher then calls out a number to identify which person will answer the multiple-choice question. For example, if the teacher calls out number 1, the pupils with their hand at the top of the pile will answer the question. If the teacher calls out number 4, then the pupils with their hand fourth in the pile will answer the question.

If a pupil answers correctly, she scores 10 points for her team colour; if she gets it wrong, she loses 5 points for her colour.

Variation

If the teacher calls, 'Shuffle,' the group members change their hand positions in the stack before the teacher shouts, 'Stop.'

Head to Head

Build knowledge and understanding.
Develop strategy and tactics.
Recognise topics under pressure (exam conditions).
Improve exam question technique.

Equipment

- Whiteboard and projector
- Exam questions and mark scheme
- Whiteboard pens

Description

Split the class into two teams and separate the chairs so that there is a large corridor down the middle of the class to reach the front whiteboard.

Select a long-answer question from an exam paper and project it on the screen. Give each team 30 seconds during which they can select words, concepts, and answers that they think will be found in the mark scheme for that question. On the start command, one pupil from each team (chosen by the team captain) runs down the corridor and starts to write on the whiteboard. They have 30 seconds to go head to head with each other and the examiner. After 30 seconds, they must put down their pens and return to their teams. The teacher now projects the mark scheme on the board. Pupils calculate how many answers they got right. Select another question and repeat the process with different pupils completing the running and writing.

Variations

Easier: Show some of the answers from the mark scheme before the discussion time begins.

Harder: Decrease or remove the discussion time so that the pupils who feel confident come straight to the board once they have read the question. In this instance, the 30-second answer time starts when the first person reaches the board.

Heads or Tails

Assess pupils' knowledge.
Encourage pupils to answer questions.

Equipment

- A coin for each pupil
- A set of questions

Description

Everyone—teacher and pupils—flips a coin and determines heads or tails. Pupils whose coin toss is the same as the teacher's once again flip their coins with the teacher. Those who again get the same result as the teacher get to answer a question from the teacher. For example, if the teacher flipped two heads in a row, those pupils who also flipped two heads are asked to answer a question. These pupils confer for an answer, and if correct, they all score 10 points. After this a new two-coin sequence starts again.

Variations

Easier: Allow the pupils who are out of the round to collaborate on an answer, but only for 5 points.

Harder: Have the pupils who are in the round pair up; the first pair to answer correctly earns all the points on offer.

Heads, Shoulders, Knees and Toes

Learn key facts.
Practice answering multiple-choice questions.

Equipment

A set of multiple-choice questions

Description

Every pupil starts the game standing up. The teacher reads a question and an answer to the class. The pupils must decide if the answer is true or false. Pupils who think the answer is true place the hands on the head, and pupils who think the answer is false place the hands on the tail (buttocks). All pupils must answer at the same time. Any pupil who answers the question correctly earns 2 points.

Variations

Easier: Pupils work in pairs and have 30 seconds to decide the answer.

Harder: Multiple-choice answers (A, B, C, and D) are provided, and the pupils must decide if the answer is A (hands on their heads), B (hands on their shoulders), C (hands on their knees), or D (hands on their toes).

High Jump

Review knowledge.
Demonstrate a range of knowledge.

Equipment

A high jump scorecard for each team (see page 39)

Description

The class is organised into teams, and each is given a high jump scorecard. For the first jump, the teacher provides a topic or category (for example, name one example of a carbohydrate), and the team has to provide one example in order to clear the bar. For the next topic or category (for instance, name two health problems associated with a high-calorie diet), the team must provide two examples in order to clear the bar.

This continues up to the maximum height of a topic, requiring 10 answers. Each team is allowed to pass at one height (they do not need to provide any answers) and is allowed to knock the bar off twice (wrong answers). Collect the scorecards to determine which team cleared the highest height.

Variations

Easier: Allow more passes for some of the teams.

Harder: Require that each team must clear each height. Allow three attempts at each height. For example, if a team must provide six answers but has only five correct answers, allow them three guesses to get the last correct answer.

High Jump Scorecard

Topic or category	Answers		Pass (put a P if you decide to pass this height)	Height cleared? (Y or N)
	1.			
	1. 2.			
	1. 2. 3.			
	1. 2.	3. 4.		
	1. 2. 3.	4. 5.		
	1. 2. 3.	4. 5. 6.		
	1. 2. 3. 4.	5. 6. 7.		
	1. 2. 3. 4.	5. 6. 7. 8.		
	1. 2. 3. 4. 5.	6. 7. 8. 9.		
	1. 2. 3. 4. 5.	6. 7. 8. 9. 10.		

From G. Long, H. Grout, and S. Taylor, 2011, *101 Classroom Games* (Champaign, IL: Human Kinetics).

Howzat!

Assess knowledge of key concepts.

Equipment

A set of questions

Description

The aim of the game is to score as many runs and lose as few wickets as possible. Begin by asking a question with as many correct answers as desired. Pupils write down as many correct answers as possible. Once everyone has written down an answer, the teacher provides all the answers that are acceptable. Pupils score a run for every correct answer they provide, but for every incorrect answer, they lose a wicket. Once they lose 10 wickets, they are out and can no longer score any more runs (but they may help another pupil). The winner is the person in the class who scores the most runs.

Variations

Easier: Play 20-20: In this variation, the teacher asks 20 questions. Allow pupils to leave a question; they will not score any runs but cannot lose a wicket, either.

Harder: Allow the pupils a maximum of six answers per question, limiting the number of possible runs to six.

I Am Not

Demonstrate a wide range of knowledge around a topic.
Improve subject-specific vocabulary.

Equipment

None

Description

This game is a twist on word description games. A pupil is given a set of keywords (such as pulmonary vein) for other pupils on her team to accurately identify. However, in this game, the pupil does this by saying what the keyword is not.

So for the example of pulmonary vein, the pupil with the keyword may say, 'I am not the aorta,' 'I am not the vena cava,' 'I am not an artery,' 'I am not the vessel that delivers deoxygenated blood to the lungs,' until his team guesses what he is. The pupil cannot say what he is, so in this example the pupil could not say, 'I am not a vein,' because he is!

Variations

Easier: Show the pupils their keywords in advance to allow some planning time.

Harder: Give a time limit (such as 45 seconds) in which to describe a set number of keywords (for instance, 3).

It's Just a Jump to the Left

Assess pupils' knowledge of facts and concepts.
Encourage pupils to attempt answers.

Equipment

A set of true-or-false questions

Description

The pupils stand in single file facing the front of the class. The space to the right of the pupils is called true, and the space to the left is called false. Begin by asking a true-or-false question and then count down, 'Three, two, one, jump.'

If the pupils think the answer is false, they must jump to their left, and if they think it's true, they must jump to their right. Pupils get 10 points if they jumped to the correct side, and then all pupils return to the centre line for the next question. The pupil who was at the front of the queue can move to the back of the line, and all the other pupils move a step forward.

Variations

Easier: Allow a longer countdown so that the pupils have more time to think about their answer. Play the pupils versus the teacher, so if the majority of the pupils has a wrong answer, the teacher gets a point.

Harder: If a pupil gets the answer wrong, he is eliminated from the game. The last remaining pupil is the winner.

Judge and Jury

Improve fact recognition.
Reinforce understanding.
Improve speaking in front of groups.
Support different points of view.

Equipment

- Three tables placed in a U-shape
- All other chairs set into lines to form a jury

Description

This game takes place in a mock courtroom arrangement. Three pupils (defendants) are given the task of convincing the others (who are acting as a jury) that their interpretation of a chosen topic is correct. Each defendant's goal is to make the jury pick his interpretation. The aim of the jury is to see through the fictitious statements and identify the correct statement.

Before setting the court in motion, get the pupils into groups of three and assign each group a topic. Give the pupils 15 minutes to decide who out of the three will be presenting the correct interpretation and who will not. During this time, the defendants should create two false interpretations of the same topic. Get the pupils to make the false interpretations as believable as possible and make sure that all three pupils have enough knowledge of their chosen topic that they can justify their statements when cross-examined by the jury.

After 15 minutes, place a team of defendants on the stand (within the U-shaped tables), and as the judge, invite each one to make a statement. After they have heard all three statements, the jury may then cross-examine each of the pupils in turn to determine the correct interpretation. A total of three questions, one per defendant, can be asked by the jury (selected by the judge).

The jury is then polled for its verdict about which version is correct. Points go to the defendants if they manage to deceive the jury; points go to the jury if they identify the correct interpretation.

Variations

Easier: Introduce barristers to defend the pupils in the dock.

Harder: Make the cross-examination more vigorous by allowing more questions.

Killer Questions

Learn key concepts and definitions.
Reinforce recall and recognition of important concepts.
Help pupils recognise strengths and weaknesses in knowledge.

Equipment

Lists of questions

Description

This game allows you to play as an individual against all your other classmates, or as teams, with the winning team being the last team still alive after answering the most questions!

Split the class into equal groups of four or five. Move the chairs and tables so that each of the teams can stand in a straight line facing the front. One person from each team steps forward as the quizmaster and stands at the front of his queue.

As with any killer-type game, the goal is to stay alive whilst eliminating all opponents. Each player has two lives; to stay alive a player must answer a question asked by the quizmaster. If she answers correctly, she moves to the back of his line. If she answers incorrectly, she takes a step forward, and the next question is offered to both the person who got the previous question wrong (player A) and the person behind her in the line (player B). Player A loses a life if player B answers a question correctly before player A does. However, if player A answers correctly before player B answers, player A keeps her life intact. Player B will still have two lives and is now asked her own question. The last pupil standing wins!

Variations

Easier: Play rapid-fire rounds with fewer people (groups of three) covering single topics.

Harder: After playing the above variation you can 'group' players depending on how well they fared. For example, all the winners join together to form a new group for the next game.

Knockout Arguments

Formulate arguments in a debate.

Equipment

- Three pieces of A4 paper and three pens
- Winner's prize (optional)
- A bell (optional)

Description

Create a boxing-style atmosphere to simulate a debate concerning a key area the pupils are studying. Inform the class of the debate topic and choose three pupils to judge the contest. Split the remainder of the class in half, with one side for the statement and the other side against it. Each side now has 30 minutes to prepare for their fight by learning key facts and concepts. Depending on the size of your class, you might need to elect three or four pupils as speakers for each side.

The fight will consist of six rounds of three minutes each. During each round, each side will argue their case by stating key facts. The teacher is the referee and steps in if the fight gets ugly! The proponent team defends and blocks their opponent's punches by throwing back a punch that counters the opponent's statement. During a round, if a team fails to provide any form of defence, then the referee can step in a give a standing count of 10. If during this time the team still fails to provide any argument, then they are knocked out and the other team wins by a knock-out! The three judges are impartial and score each round based on who they believe provided the best argument during that particular round.

Variations

Easier: Provide each team with key facts to support their argument.

Harder: Inform the class of the debate ahead of time, but do not tell them what side they will be arguing for. They must attend the next lesson prepared to argue for either side.

Ladders

Prepare a timeline.
Recall and recognise information.

Equipment

- Chairs
- A4 cards

Description

This is an easy game that uses minimal classroom furniture. As in the game of musical chairs, set up a number of chairs facing back to back in two lines. Make sure that the number of chairs in each line represents the number of answers that are required to complete the sequence that you have chosen. Split the group into two teams, making sure that the team sizes match the number of chairs.

Each pupil is given a word written on an A4 card. The teacher can select any topic that offers a sequence, for instance, an historical timeline or the anatomical components an oxygen molecule travels through from the mouth to the lungs. With the start command, pupils arrange themselves in the correct sequence, sitting in their chairs. The first team to finish in the correct sequence is the winner.

Variations

Easier: To simulate an exam technique, offer more possible answers than chairs and ask the pupils to select and justify where they start based on your question.

Harder: Give a short period of decision-making time when no one is allowed to be seated; on your command, teams sit as quickly as possible.

Last Past the Finish Line

Learn key concepts and definitions.
Practice short answers to questions.
Work on recall and response.

Equipment

A set of questions

Description

In this game the goal is to not get to the finish line (which is a score of 10). Playing as individuals or teams, pupils answer questions asked by the teacher. If a pupil (or team) gets an answer wrong, he gets a point and moves closer to the finish line. It is up to you whether this is done physically or metaphorically! The pupils that answer correctly stay where they are. When pupils have 10 incorrect answers, they have reached the finish line and are eliminated. The last person still playing is the winner.

Variations

Easier: If players pass the finish line and are eliminated, they can join other teams, or if possible, write more questions. Have themes or categories of questions that the pupils can select from.

Harder: Make the questions harder after each round of questions.

Let's Get Ready to Tumble

Assess pupils' knowledge.
Gain familiarity with examination questions.

Equipment

- Children's building blocks
- Sets of questions (examination papers or pupil-generated questions)

Description

The purpose of this game is to cause a tower of building blocks to crash to the floor!

Two teams take turns asking each other a series of questions. If team A gets a question wrong, team B hands them a block that they have to add to the tower. If team A gets the question correct, then they give a block to team B to add to the same tower. Play continues until the tower collapses. Whichever team caused the tower to tumble to the ground loses the game.

Variations

Easier: Use questions with only one correct answer or use multiple-choice questions.

Harder: Start with the tower already partly built.

Lie Detectors

Recognise and recall information.
Improve understanding of concepts and topics.
Develop reasoning and justification skills.

Equipment

Key resources, such as textbooks or reference books

Description

Give each pupil a concept or topic to individually research; they then write a short description (roughly a paragraph) about it. They must write the description with accuracy; however, they should also hide, as cleverly as possible, five inaccurate pieces of information within the description.

Each pupil takes a turn reading her description aloud to the class whilst the other pupils act as lie detectors trying to identify the five inaccurate pieces of information. Once the pupils have had a chance to write their answers, the teacher explores how many of the five lies the pupils think they have identified. This is then clarified with the pupil who read the description.

Each pupil earns a point for the correct identification of each lie. The reader's scores are based on the number of lies not found. For instance, if the highest number of correctly identified lies was two, the pupil who read the description would earn 3 points, the number of lies not identified.

Variations

Easier: Assign the written description as homework and post it on the school's Intranet or Web site so that other pupils can play the game from home.

Harder: Obtain longer descriptions by assigning broader topics or concepts to cover, similar to a long essay question.

Make It, Draw It or Mime It

Learn key concepts and definitions.
Encourage creative communication.

Equipment

- Children's plasticine or modeling clay
- Whiteboard pens
- A set of keyword cards
- A set of instruction cards (see page 51)

Description

Decide on the competition format that you wish to use. You can split the class into two teams, have pairs of pupils compete against one another, or have one pupil compete against the rest of the class. Decide on extra rules, such as the number of guesses allowed, and a time limit, if any.

The two sets of cards (keyword cards and instruction cards) are laid out face down. Pupils first select a keyword card and then select an instruction card. The instruction card tells them what method they can use to provide keyword clues for their team. The goal is to make, draw, or mime clues to help the team guess the keyword. For example, if the keyword is biceps and the instruction card is 'Draw it,' then the pupil must attempt to draw a picture that will help his team or partner guess correctly.

Variations

Easier: Allow three pupils to come to the front of the class and make, draw or mime the same keyword simultaneously.

Harder: Use definition cards so that the pupil has to know what is being described on the card in order to be able to make, draw or mime it.

Make It, Draw It or Mime It Cards

Make it!	Make it!
Make it!	Make it!
Draw it!	Draw it!
Draw it!	Draw it!
Mime it!	Mime it!
Mime it!	Mime it!

From G. Long, H. Grout, and S. Taylor, 2011, *101 Classroom Games* (Champaign, IL: Human Kinetics).

Marbles

Learn key concepts.
Extend answers and develop arguments.

Equipment

- Pack of marbles (with newspaper and different colours of insulating tape, it is possible to build your own marbles)
- A jack
- A measuring tape

Description

This game can be played individually in groups of two or more, or pupils can compete in teams of two or more. An area eight metres long and two metres wide is required for each game. One end is the starting line. Each individual or team has a coloured marble to use for the game. The jack is placed six metres away from the starting line.

The first pupil or team is given a question to answer or a statement to argue (for a maximum of 10 marks). The teacher scores the answer. The number of marks awarded for the answer or the argument is then exchanged for pigeon steps. For example, if the pupil achieves six marks, she can take six pigeon steps from the starting line towards the jack.

The pupil then throws her marble from her new starting position and tries to land it as near to the jack as possible. After this is completed, pupil or team two has their go. A point is awarded for the marbles nearest the jack. The number of marbles per person or team can vary, as can the number of rounds the game is played. The winner is the person or team whose marble is nearest the jack.

Variations

Easier: Provide resources to assist the pupil answering the question.

Harder: Any incorrect answers result in the pupils having to take steps backwards.

Missing Links

Develop recall and recognition skills.
Review keywords.
Learn definitions.

Equipment

- Whiteboard or projector
- Board pens

Description

Based on the game show Blockbusters, this game can be played individually or in teams. Fill the grid (see following figure for an example) with the first letter of each of the keywords that you wish your pupils to be able to recognise from a clue. Create the questions or clues for each letter by making a glossary for your chosen topic area.

Players take turns selecting a letter from the grid and responding to the question or clue offered by the teacher. When players answer correctly, the cell for the letter they chose is coloured in with the team's colours. Their goal is to move from one side of the grid to the other, or from the top to the bottom, before their opponents do by colouring adjacent cells.

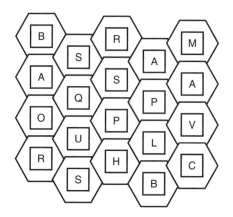

Variations

Easier: Allow the pupils to have a glossary with them as they play the game.

Harder: Get your pupils to each create their own 'missing links' game for two other pupils to play.

Number Minefield

Improve exam-taking technique.
Improve recall and interpretation.

Equipment

- Chairs spaced around the classroom
- Dartboard (real or virtual from Internet)
- Dartboard number cards
- Reusable adhesive

Description

This game is based on the numbers that are found on a dartboard. Place each of these numbers on a card and randomly stick a number to the underside of each chair. Spread the chairs out throughout the classroom so that there is space for the pupils to move freely between them.

Create exam-style questions requiring a slightly longer answer. Project one onto a whiteboard or read it to the pupils. The pupils then have 10 seconds to move around the room, in and out of the chairs, composing an answer to the question in their heads. When the 10 seconds are up, they choose a chair to sit on. Once they are seated, throw a dart, striking a number on the dartboard (do this either using a real dartboard or an online virtual board). Ask the pupils to reach under their seats to see whose number corresponds to that thrown on the dartboard. That pupil stands and offers the answer. A full and correct answer gets the pupil the number of points struck by the dart. A half answer gets the number of points thrown by the dart divided by two. A new question is asked, and the game continues, with the pupils keeping their own individual score.

Variations

Easier: Rather than stating a question before the pupils' movement, give the question blind, after the dart has chosen the pupil who will answer. This way you can choose the question based on the pupil who has been randomly selected.

Harder: Once a number has been selected by the dart, take it out of the game, therefore reducing the number of seats.

Our Survey Says . . .

Learn key concepts.
Identify the most important answers to an examination question.

Equipment

A set of five-mark questions and answers

Description

This game is based on the popular game show Family Fortunes. Prepare a set of questions and five correct answers for each question. Assign points for each of the five answers (so they add up to 100).

Examples

Name five reasons for taking part in sport.

Name five barriers to sporting participation that exist for women.

Read the question to the pupils and have them write five answers. Reveal the points available for each answer and have pupils add up their points.

Variations

Easier: Provide the pupils with 8-10 answers (only 5 of which are correct); they have to select the top 5 answers.

Harder: Have pupils work in teams of five (as a family). Have one person at a time answer the question so it becomes harder to answer the question as answers are eliminated.

Overtake

Recap and review previous work.
Assess pupils' knowledge.
Answer questions whilst under pressure.

Equipment

An object for the pupils to pass around

Description

The class sits in a circle facing inwards. One pupil (player A) is randomly selected to start. The teacher asks him a question (for example, name five countries that begin with a vowel, or name five animals). The pupil to the left of the selected pupil (player B) is given the object, and as soon as the teacher finishes the question, he begins passing the object around the circle to the left. The challenge is for player A to complete the answer before the object gets back to player B. (Instruct the pupil to the right of player A to pass the object around player A to player B).

If player A is able to complete the answer, then the pupil holding the object when player A finishes must answer the next question.

Variations

Easier: If the object is dropped, it must return back to the start of the circle.

Harder: Award player A points for each member of the circle who didn't get to hold the object. (The faster they complete the answer, the more points they would get!)

Pairs

Reinforce key concepts.
Improve recall and recognition.
Review keywords.
Learn definitions.

Equipment

- A4 paper
- Pens
- Glossary

Description

The task in this game is to match a keyword to a definition. Make a glossary-style list on paper and cut it to separate the keywords from their definitions. Place the individual slips of paper upside down on the table and ask each pupil to turn over two pieces. If the two are a pair—a keyword and its definition—the pupil gets to keep the pair. If it is not a pair, then the pupil places each piece back where it came from in the upside-down position. The next pupil has a go. The goal is to collect as many pairs as possible.

Variations

Easier: Turn over the definitions, and the pupils only have to find the keyword.

Harder: Have a short time limit for choosing and reading the two pieces so that the pupil feels under exam-like pressure. Delete some words in the definitions to make recognizing the keyword harder.

Pass It On

Learn keywords.
Demonstrate a range of knowledge.

Equipment

A set of questions

Description

Pupils play this game in groups of four or more. Each pupil begins the game with five lives. Pupils decide who will go first (this varies for each game). Provide a topic or question (one that has numerous correct answers) to the group. The first pupil must provide from one to three keywords for this topic or one to three correct answers to the question. The pupils answer in a clockwise direction. If the first pupil answers with

- one correct answer, the next pupil in the circle has to give her answer;
- two correct answers, the direction of the circle is reversed; and the next pupil has to provide an answer;
- three correct answers, the pupil next in the circle is skipped, and the pupil next to the one skipped provides the next answer.

If a pupil cannot provide an answer, then she loses one life, and the last pupil to answer earns a life. When a pupil loses a life, a new topic or question is provided and the game resumes.

Variations

Easier: Pupils have one lifeline; if they are unable to answer the question, they may pass.

Harder: Introduce the rule that pupils earn a life every time they provide three answers.

Peek, Copy, All In or Save

Assess the class's knowledge and understanding.

Equipment

- Answer cards or A4 whiteboards
- Lifeline cards (see page 60)

Description

This game is based on the game show Are You Smarter Than a Ten-Year-Old? The class plays against the teacher! One pupil is selected at random to represent the class, whilst the remaining pupils each have an answer card (A4 whiteboards do the job). The pupils must use these to write their answers to every question. The selected pupil has to earn 10 points for the class to beat the teacher. Every correct answer given is worth 1 point. If the pupil does not know the answer, he can choose one of three lifelines (Peek, Copy, or All In).

Peek: This means that another pupil is selected at random to reveal his answer on his paper or whiteboard. The original pupil can decide to use this answer or go with one of his own. This lifeline can be used twice.

Copy: As previously, another pupil is selected at random, but this time the pupil's answer must be used. This lifeline can also be used twice.

All in: This time the entire class has to show their answers, and the pupil can use this information to come up with an answer. This lifeline can also be used twice. If the pupil gives an incorrect answer to a question, he has a lifeline (save) but it can be used only once.

Save: As with Copy, a pupil is selected at random, and his answer must be correct in order for the original pupil to stay in the game (and not let the teacher win!)

Variations

Easier: Give the pupils two lives. If they get an answer wrong, they can play one of their lives.

Harder: Allow the pupils only one lifeline for each category, so that they have to at least attempt some answers they may not be sure of.

Lifeline Cards

PEEK LIFELINE 1 By using this card you can look at one of your classmates' answers. This classmate is selected at random. You do not have to use their answer.	**PEEK LIFELINE 2** By using this card you can look at one of your classmates' answers. This classmate is selected at random. You do not have to use their answer.
COPY LIFELINE 1 By using this card you can look at one of your classmates' answers. This classmate is selected at random. You **must** use their answer.	**COPY LIFELINE 2** By using this card you can look at one of your classmates' answers. This classmate is selected at random. You **must** use their answer.
ALL-IN LIFELINE 1 By using this card you can look at all of your classmates' answers. You can use this information to choose your answer.	**ALL-IN LIFELINE 2** By using this card you can look at all of your classmates' answers. You can use this information to choose your answer.
SAVE LIFELINE 1 This card can only be used if you have just provided an incorrect answer. By using this card you can look at one of your classmates' answers. This classmate is selected at random. You **must** use their answer. It must be correct for you to stay in the game!	

From G. Long, H. Grout, and S. Taylor, 2011, *101 Classroom Games* (Champaign, IL: Human Kinetics).

Penalty Shootout

Learn key concepts.
Increase confidence in answering.

Equipment

Penalty shootout scorecard (see page 62)

Description

This game relies on having confidence in your knowledge. Pupils are paired and compete against each other. Each pair decides who will be the striker and who will be the goalkeeper. The teacher will ask a question or provide a statement, such as 'Name as many countries as you can that begin with the letter B.' The striker has 30 seconds to indicate how many correct answers she can provide. The goalkeeper then decides if she knows more answers than the striker; if not, she may allow the striker to attempt the penalty. The outcome of the penalty is as follows:

Striker states the highest number and correctly answers.   GOAL

Goalkeeper states the highest number and correctly
     answers.   SAVE

Striker states the highest number and incorrectly
     answers.   SAVE

Goalkeeper states the highest number and incorrectly
     answers.   GOAL

A penalty shootout is best of five, and if the pair is tied after five attempts each, they go to sudden death.

Variations

Easier: The striker and goalkeeper take turns answering questions. If they answer correctly, they either score or save the penalty.

Harder: Play two players or teams against one goalkeeper.

Penalty Shootout Scorecard

KEY:

G = goal

S = save

	1	2	3	4	5	Winner
Striker						
Goal-keeper						

	1	2	3	4	5	Winner
Striker						
Goal-keeper						

	1	2	3	4	5	Winner
Striker						
Goal-keeper						

	1	2	3	4	5	Winner
Striker						
Goal-keeper						

From G. Long, H. Grout, and S. Taylor, 2011, *101 Classroom Games* (Champaign, IL: Human Kinetics).

Phone a Friend

Work on key concepts and definitions.
Introduce research skills.

Equipment

The Internet

Description

This is a good game to play if your lesson is in a computer room. The class is split into teams of four; one pupil is captain and the other three are friends. The teacher asks the captains a question, and they have a set time to provide an answer. The captain can write down the answer himself or nominate a friend to help him.

Friend one is on a computer and can use the Internet to search for the answer; friend two has his class notes to help him find the answer; and friend three is allowed to discuss possible answers with the captain. The game lasts for eight questions, but each friend is only allowed to be nominated twice during the game.

Variations

Easier: All three friends try to find the answer, and all can suggest an answer to the captain.

Harder: Friends may be nominated just once each during the game.

Pick and Mix

Learn key concepts.
Understand how examination questions are written.
Quickly scan information.

Equipment

- A4 paper
- Reusable adhesive
- Pens

Description

Each pupil is provided with two pieces of A4 paper. Provide each pupil with an answer that they must keep secret. On one piece of A4 paper, pupils write the answer they have just been given, and on the other piece of A4 paper, they write a question relevant to the answer or a description of what the answer is.

Pupils can use their textbooks for this task because it is very important they write down a suitable and correct question or description. Each pupil should then fold up the piece of paper that provides the question or description and place it in a bag with all the other descriptions.

Each of the answers should be stuck around the classroom walls. The teacher then asks every pupil to draw a description or question from the bag, waiting until the starting whistle before unfolding it. Once every pupil has a piece of paper, the teacher blows the whistle (or indicates the start of the game), and pupils open their papers and read the description or question. As quickly as possible, they must then find the correct answer on the wall and stand beside it.

Points are awarded to each pupil standing by the correct answer. All the descriptions are then refolded and placed back into the bag, and the whole process starts again.

Variations

Easier: Pupils are given a question instead of an answer and write the answer to the question instead.

Harder: Give extra points to the first pupil to stand by the correct answer.

Picture Perfect

Assess pupils' understanding of key concepts.
Encourage pupils to explain key concepts.
Encourage pupils to think on their feet.

Equipment

A set of keywords or topics and related pictures

Description

The class is split into teams, and all pupils stand together in their teams. The teacher introduces a topic (for example, the human body) and then shows the first picture. A pupil from team A steps forward and relates the picture to the topic. If she is successful, then the next picture is shown, and a pupil from team B will step forward. The pictures can range from having literal relevance to the topic (a picture of blood cells; so therefore the pupil could describe the functions of red and white blood cells) to a more abstract connection (a picture of a bicycle pump; in this case, the pupil may talk about the heart being a pump or she may talk about how the lungs increase in size when we breathe in and take in air). The teacher awards points to the teams for a successful explanation. When the pictures have finished, the teacher can begin a new topic.

Variations

Easier: Include some words on the picture that may help the pupils to talk about the picture.

Harder: Keep the picture up for a set period of time so if one pupil has run out of things to say, a teammate can then step forward to ensure that the time is filled.

Pin the Tail on the . . .

Reinforce key concepts and definitions.
Improve recall and recognition.

Equipment

- Coloured paper
- Reusable adhesive or sticky dots
- Blindfold

Description

Place keywords randomly on a whiteboard or a large chalkboard. Create a question based on each keyword (for instance, the word anxiety would have a question based on the topic of anxiety).

Split the class into small teams. Each team is designated a colour and provided with small strips of coloured card (like a marker) with a piece of adhesive or a sticky dot on one side. Taking turns, a member of each team comes to the whiteboard and puts on the blindfold. They are then spun round five times one way and then the other. (Make sure that the area is clear and free from furniture so that the players cannot injure themselves.) Once stopped, the player is directed to the board where he must affix his team's colour marker. The team is asked the question nearest the marker. Use a simple point system for answers.

Variations

Easier: Repeat keywords so that the teams can use the answers from previous questions to help them.

Harder: Use a roll-over point system; when a team answers incorrectly, or they pass on their question, the next team has the points added to theirs.

Pool Championships

Learn key concepts.
Practice for a variety of examination answers.

Equipment

- Photocopies of a pool table for each pair (see page 68)
- A set of examination questions

Description

Put the pupils in pairs and provide one photocopy of the pool table to each pair. Have the pairs decide who will pot first by tossing a coin. The first player chooses any ball to pot. She can attempt to pot either the spots or stripes. If she answers correctly, she pots the ball. She is then limited to that ball type (spots or stripes) in further shots. The potted ball is crossed out on the sheet. If she answers incorrectly, the second player still can decide to go for spots or stripes. Players take turns choosing balls to pot and answering questions. The difficulty of each question will depend on the difficulty of the shot.

Spots

Ball 7 = 1-mark question
Ball 2 = 1-mark question
Ball 1 = 2-mark question
Ball 4 = 3-mark question
Ball 5 = 4-mark question

Stripes

Ball 10 = 1-mark question
Ball 11 = 1-mark question
Ball 15 = 2-mark question
Ball 14 = 3-mark question
Ball 9 = 4-mark question
Black ball = 5-mark question

If a player answers correctly, she attempts another pot. If she answers incorrectly, the other player attempts her pot. Once a player has potted all five of her balls, she can attempt to pot the black ball. The first person to pot the black ball wins.

Variations

Easier: Make each question worth one mark and the black ball worth two.

Harder: Players can attempt a plant shot and pot two balls at once. For instance, potting ball 14 and 9 together (3 plus 4) would be a 7-mark question. (Limit players to one plant shot per frame.)

Pool Championships

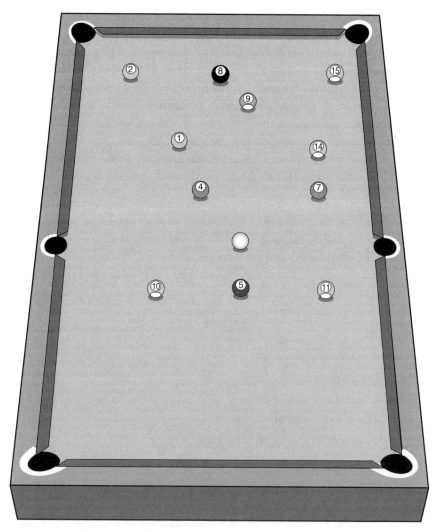

From G. Long, H. Grout, and S. Taylor, 2011, *101 Classroom Games* (Champaign, IL: Human Kinetics).

Post-it Note Scramble

Learn key concepts and definitions.
Assess pupils' knowledge.
Scan information quickly.

Equipment

- Post-it notes, each with a keyword written on it
- A glossary or list of definitions

Description

Stick the Post-it notes randomly on the whiteboard. Pupils are put into teams, and as in Family Fortunes, one member of each team stands with his back to the board.

The teacher or another pupil describes one of the words, and when he has finished, the two pupils have to turn around, locate and quickly grab the correct answer. The winning team is the team with the most Post-it notes at the end of the game.

Variations

Easier: You may let other members of the class call out the answer after three seconds have passed.

Harder: Don't allow the pupil reading out the definitions to have a glossary, so he also has to demonstrate his understanding.

Puzzled

Learn key concepts and definitions.
Understand examination questions and answers.
Work with different pupils.

Equipment

- Paper with either examination questions or keywords
- Stopwatch

Description

Pupils are each given a piece of paper that they must keep hidden from others until the game begins. The pupils will either have a keyword written on their papers or an examination question. As soon as the time starts, the pupils have to quickly move around, looking at the other pupils' words, trying to group themselves so that they have one exam question and all the correct answers for that question. For example, the pupil with the question 'What are the colours of the French flag?' would have to find one pupil with the word red, another pupil with the word blue, and another with the word white to complete the task (during that time, those with the answers will have been looking for a question that matches their answer). Pupils are not allowed to talk, and they earn points for completing their group in a set period.

Variations

Easier: Allow pupils to talk after 30 seconds have passed.

Harder: Make some of the words closely linked to more than one of the questions so that the pupils have to decide which question is more relevant.

Question Ball

Learn key concepts and definitions.
Assess pupils' knowledge.
Develop confidence.

Equipment

- A set of questions
- A ball or beanbag

Description

All the pupils stand. Start the game by asking a question and throwing the ball or beanbag to one of the pupils. If the pupil catches the ball, she attempts to answer the question. If she answers incorrectly, or drops the ball, she throws the ball to another pupil (who must try and answer the original question) and the first pupil has to sit down. But if the question is answered correctly, she stays standing. The teacher then asks another question, and the pupil who has just answered the question throws the ball to another pupil. When a pupil answers a question incorrectly, the pupils sitting down can put their hands up, and if one of them can answer the question, she can stand up and rejoin the game.

Variations

Easier: If a pupil doesn't know an answer, she can select one of the pupils sitting down to help him.

Harder: Play until a set number of pupils (perhaps five) are left standing.

55

Question Conkers

Assess pupils' knowledge of facts and concepts.

Equipment

A set of quick-fire questions

Description

A third of the class are the quizmasters or referees. They are each given a set of questions (or they write their own), and then they spread themselves around the classroom.

Two pupils stand by one of the question masters and face each other, ready to answer a question. The first pupil to answer correctly wins the points and scores, as in a game of Conkers. The pupils then separate and move on to find another opponent and another quizmaster. The winner is the highest scoring conker after a set period of time.

Those of you who are not familiar with the scoring of Conkers, read the following:

All pupils (conkers) begin the game as none-ers, meaning that they have conquered no one yet. If a none-er breaks another none-er, then he becomes a one-er; if he was a one-er, then he becomes a two-er, and so on. So if a pupil gets the first question right before his opponent does, he will become a one-er whilst his opponent stays as a none-er.

The winning conker (pupil) acquires both the previous score of the losing conker (pupil), and the score from that particular game. For example, if a two-er plays a three-er, the winning conker (pupil) will become a six-er (the two previous scores plus one for the current game). Therefore, the losing conker (pupil) goes back to being a none-er.

Variations

Easier: Allow the pupils multiple attempts at getting the correct answer—do not limit them to their original answer.

Harder: If pupils lose three contests in a row, they are out of the game.

Quizzical Chairs

Answer true or false questions.

Equipment

- One chair per pupil
- A set of true and false statements
- Music

Description

This game is a modified version of the classic party game Musical Chairs. Place the chairs in a line across the classroom (one chair for each pupil).

While the music is playing, the pupils circulate clockwise around the chairs. When the music stops, the teacher reads a statement. If a pupil believes that a statement is true, she quickly sits down on a chair. Any pupil who answers a statement incorrectly is eliminated, and a chair is removed from the game.

Variations

Easier: Write four statements (a, b, c, d) on the board and inform the pupils that three are true. When the teacher starts to read a statement they believe is false, they sit down.

Harder: If the majority of the pupils are answering questions correctly, then you can impose a rule that the last person to sit for a correct answer is eliminated.

Racing Cars

Learn key concepts.
Teach the benefits of answering questions.

Equipment

A set of questions

Description

This game works well in groups of six or more. Five of the pupils are race car drivers, and one is the race official (who reads the questions). To begin, the race official provides the rest of the group (the drivers) with a topic (for example, volcanoes). Each driver has one minute to write as many keywords associated with that topic. The race lineup is determined by the number of correct words written down by each driver. The driver with the most correct words associated with the topic is in the pole position, and the remaining drivers line up accordingly in single file. The race itself is a set number of laps (questions).

The race official asks a question, and the first driver to raise his hand gets to answer the question. If he gets the answer right, he overtakes the driver in front of him (if this is the pupil in pole position, he remains in first place). If the answer is incorrect, the pupil spins out and moves to the back of the race. If a question is unanswered, the race official can award a pit stop, giving the drivers 45 seconds to find the answer in their books. The winner of the race is the driver at the front of the line after the designated number of questions has been asked and answered.

Variations

Easier: Increase the number of pit stops.
Harder: After three spin outs, the driver crashes out of the race.

Randomizer

Recap key concepts.
Encourage group learning.

Equipment

- A hat
- A beanbag or ball, a different colour for each team
- A set of questions

Description

Pupils are organised into four to six teams with each team represented by a colour. The game is conducted somewhat like a traditional quiz game. The teacher reads out (or shows) a question that will need to be answered soon and then allows the teams a set period of time to discuss the possible answers amongst themselves. Before the question is answered the teacher (without looking) pulls out two coloured beanbags from the hat. The first colour drawn from the hat designates the team that will get to answer the question; if the team is correct, they will earn 10 points, and the second team has 10 points deducted from their score. If, however, the first team is incorrect, they lose 10 points, and the second team gets the chance to answer the question correctly for the 10 points.

Variations

Easier: If the first team's members are unsure of the answer, allow them to ask another team (not the team drawn second from the hat) for help. The two teams earn 5 points each for a correct answer.

Harder: Do not read out the question before selecting the teams and allow the second team to choose the category or the topic of the question.

Red Herrings

Assess pupils' knowledge.
Familiarise pupils with examination answers.

Equipment

A set of questions and their answers

Description

The class is organised into teams. Team A is shown an examination question and a list of associated answers. In amongst the correct answers, the teacher has added some incorrect answers (red herrings). Team A gets awarded a point for each correct answer they select, but lose all their points and their turn if they select an incorrect one. Team A can stop at any time and bank their points. When they have finished, team B is shown the next question.

Variations

Easier: Allow the teams a lifeline (the teacher reveals one of the incorrect answers).

Harder: Add as many incorrect answers as there are correct answers.

Red or Black

Practice answering exam questions.

Equipment

- A black or red number card for each pupil
- A set of questions

Description

Divide the class into a red team and a black team. Each pupil is given a red or black number card (depending on the team) that he fastens to his jumper. (Bibs with numbers would also work.)

The pupils then stand in a circle and link arms, alternating red and black. The teacher (or another pupil) stands in the middle of the circle and slowly spins, with eyes shut and one arm outstretched, whilst the circle of pupils rotates slowly anti-clockwise. When the teacher says stop, the pupils stop rotating, and whomever the teacher is pointing to (for instance, red 6) has to answer a question. If red 6 gets the question correct, he earns points equal to his number for his team (red 6 would earn 6 points for the red team).

Variations

Easier: Allow the teams to confer for half the points (if red 6 has to ask his team for the answer, he would score 3 points).

Harder: Let the pupils choose their own numbers before the game begins. Then link the difficulty of the question to the team member's number card: pupils with numbers from 1 to 12 would get easy questions, those with numbers 13 to 24 would get moderately hard questions, and those with 25 to 36 would get difficult questions.

Relay Runners

Learn key concepts and definitions.
Work on recall and response time.

Equipment

20 definition cards (see following examples)

<table>
<tr>
<td>

Definition: (this definition should match the keyword written on the bottom of the final card)
Keyword: (this should match the definition at the top of the next card)

</td>
<td>

Definition: (this definition should match the keyword written on the bottom of the previous card)
Keyword: (this should match the definition at the top of the next card)

</td>
</tr>
</table>

Description

Teams of four each stand a short distance away from a table where their definition cards are shuffled and spread out face up.

Runner one (one from each team) runs to the table, picks up a card, and brings it back to number two. At the bottom of the card is a word or concept from the topic specified. Runner two has to run to the table and find the card that has the corresponding definition. She brings this back to runner three who now has a new word at the bottom of her card for which she must find the definition. Remind pupils that the card with the definition matching their word may already have been collected by another team member. They will need to check those cards as well in order to find the match. This continues until all cards have been collected. The first team to collect all the cards and lay them out so they connect and make sense wins.

Variations

Easier: Use different numbers of definition cards for different outcomes: For instance, use 5 cards for a quick-fire starter or plenary game, or 15 cards for an end-of-lesson test.

Harder: Use variations of words, sentences, and even incomplete sentences as the concepts related to the definition to be found.

Remember My Name

Introduce memory techniques.
Break the ice for new groups or classes.
Assess existing knowledge on a newly introduced topic.

Equipment

- An A4-sized answer card for each pupil
- A set of questions

Description

Each pupil is given a card with the answer to one of the forthcoming questions (for example, Paris). For the first five minutes of the lesson, the pupils walk around, meet, and talk to as many other pupils as possible. The goal is to connect each classmate's name with the words on his card (thus Richard is Paris, Anna is London, and so on). The pupils must try to help their classmates remember their word; Richard may speak with a French accent and stand as tall as possible to resemble the Eiffel Tower in order to help his classmates remember that he has the Paris card.

At the end of the five minutes, the pupils sit down and the test begins. For each question the teacher reads, the pupils must answer with a classmate's name. For example, the answer to the question 'What is the capital of France?' would be Richard.

Variations

Easier: Allow the pupils half points if they can't remember the classmate's name but know the answer to the question.

Harder: Put more than one word on pupils' cards (such as biceps, triceps, flexion). This may be used to encourage memory techniques for answers that require more detail.

Remember, Remember

Work on recall and sequencing.
Teach how to chunk information (memory technique).
Practice performance under pressure (exam conditions).

Equipment

- Chairs placed in a circle
- Category prompt cards

Description

This game is based purely on the pupils' ability to remember and recall information. Sit the pupils in groups of five or six in a circle. The teacher places a pile of prompt cards face down in the centre of the circle. Each card has a single category word (for instance, rivers) that acts as a prompt to get the pupils to state a keyword that relates to the category.

One pupil turns over a card for all to see and says, 'to my left (or right) …' and a word that relates to that category. The person in the chosen direction must say another word from the original category followed by the word that was given by the first pupil. The next person in the chosen direction must say a new word followed by the second and the first pupil's word, and so on. If a pupil gives a wrong answer, recites the sequence incorrectly, or has to pass, she loses one of her three lives. If she loses all of her lives, she is given a sheet with keywords from the current topic to review whilst the game continues. The game ends when either all players have lost their lives or all the keywords from that category have been covered.

Another pupil then turns over a new category prompt card, selects a direction, and starts the game again.

Variations

Easier: Offer all the pupils the opportunity, before the round being played, to review from sheets containing the keywords from each category.

Harder: Increase or decrease the group size to change the number of times each pupil is called on to give a keyword.

Review Tennis

Learn key concepts and definitions.
Practice recall and response.

Equipment

A set of questions

Description

Players

This game allows pupils to play as individuals in a number of different formats.

- Singles: played 1v1, with an umpire
- Team Singles: played 1v1 but with each player in the team rotating in
- Doubles: 2v2, with an umpire (each player taking alternate turns)
- Mixed Doubles: 2v2, with an umpire (any player from a team answering)
- Team knockout: any size teams, with an umpire, where the first to enter the court can play

Court Space

Depending on the number of players taking part, make sure that the players are faced opposite each other with a net (chairs or table) between them. If the whole class is involved, move all furniture to the sides, allowing for a Wimbledon centre-court atmosphere to be produced. Whatever the setup, the umpire must always be seated at one end of the net.

Scoring

Decide who is to serve first by using a killer question, tossing a coin, or any other means you prefer. Once that has been decided, the umpire starts the rally with a question. The questions should allow for more than one possible correct answer. Each player, depending on the selected format, answers in turn. The rally ends when the players run out of possible answers or one player answers incorrectly.

Points are awarded using the tennis scoring system.

Variations

Easier: Offer chances to play a *smash* card that ends a rally without having to answer. (Limit to one per team or individual per set; do not allow one to be used on set point!)

Harder: Have a *killer word* for each question, a word that wins the rally for the player who uses it.

River Crossing

Reinforce key concepts.

Equipment

(All are optional and can be swapped for something similar):

- A4 paper
- Crates or chairs
- Towels
- A set of questions

Description

This game will rely on pupils working together as a team and making appropriate decisions. The challenge is for each team to win as much equipment as possible in order to cross the river (the classroom) without touching the floor. Each piece of equipment is worth a certain number of points:

A4 paper	1 point (easy questions)
Crate or chair	5 points (moderately difficult questions)
Towels	10 points (hard questions)

The challenge for each team is to decide what combination of questions they must answer to win enough equipment to get their team across the classroom: Will many easy questions be sufficient or must they answer a few hard questions as well? A good idea is to have a set time period in which the teams take it in turns choosing their question type and trying to successfully provide the correct answer in order to win the relevant equipment.

Once all the questions have been answered, each team tries to cross the classroom using the equipment they have won. No pupil is allowed to touch the classroom floor. The team that travels farthest across the classroom is the winner.

Variations

Easier: Allow pupils three lifelines that give them one minute to use their textbooks.

Harder: Permit only one person from the team to answer a question at a time.

Rock, Paper, Scissors

Practice answering exam questions.
Increase familiarity with exam mark schemes.

Equipment

- Past exam papers and mark schemes
- Paper
- Music

Description

Give the pupils access to a range of past exam papers and the relevant mark schemes. Allow them 5 to 10 minutes to choose three questions that they think they would find hard. The pupils write down the three questions and the answers. They then label one question the rock question, one the paper question, and the final one the scissors question.

The purpose of the game is for the pupils to score as many points as they can within the time limit. The pupils walk around the classroom to music and when the music stops, they randomly pair up. They play a game of rock, paper, scissors, and the winner gets to answer a question posed by the loser. The question asked depends on how the winner won the game of rock, paper, scissors. For instance, if he won by playing the rock, he must answer the question that the loser designated a rock. If he answers correctly, he scores a point. After the answer (right or wrong), both pupils find another pupil and begin the game again. Pupils keep track of the number of points they earn.

Variations

Easier: If the game of rock, paper, scissors ends in a draw, both players get to answer a question.

Harder: If a player answers incorrectly (player A), he then asks his opponent (player B) a question; if player B is correct, he (player B) earns 2 points.

Roll With It

Assess pupils' knowledge.
Evaluate a range of understanding of a topic.
Help pupils learn in a group.

Equipment

- A set of questions
- One die per team

Description

The class is organised into teams (from two to six pupils per team). The teacher asks a question with multiple correct answers (for instance, name the states of Australia). Each team then rolls a die to determine how many answers their team needs to provide (for instance, if their team rolls a four, then they must name four Australian states). If the team is able to meet their number, they score that many points; any fewer and they score 0. The teacher then asks another question, and the teams roll their die again.

Variations

Easier: Allow the team to roll their die again if they think they cannot get all the answers. (Warn them, however, that they may roll a higher number!)

Harder: If a team rolls a one, they must roll again.

Run Around

Learn key concepts and definitions.
Improve recall and recognition.
Practice multiple-choice questions.

Equipment

- Cones or markers
- Signs or labels
- Lists of questions

Description

Mark out three areas in the sports hall labelled A, B and C. Start with the pupils in the centre of the room and ask all of them a multiple-choice question along with the answer options A, B and C. At this point, pupils begin to move to the area the represents the correct answer. However, until the teacher gives an audible signal, the pupils may try to trick the others. They may not run to the correct area straight away; they can fake the others during this time. However, on the teacher's signal, pupils then have a limited time to get to the real answer. The pupils who answered correctly score points for getting it right, and these points are based on how many pupils got it wrong (e.g., if A were the correct answer, and there were 15 pupils standing in areas B and C, all those pupils standing in A get 15 points each). After a question, all the pupils go back to the centre of the room.

Variations

Easier: Offer more than just A, B and C options.

Harder: Change the time available to run around.

Sabotage

Learn key concepts and definitions.
Assess pupils' knowledge.
Give pupils confidence in their understanding.

Equipment

A set of questions

Description

This game takes a bit of preplanning since three or four pupils need to be given advance instructions. The lesson before the game takes place, tell three or four selected pupils that they will each be assigned to a team, but that their objective will be to secretly sabotage their team by suggesting incorrect answers to the questions asked. They are not allowed to overrule what is written on the paper, but they should appear confident of their wrong answer in order to mislead their team. On lesson day, have the teams collaborate to take a written quiz. At the end of the quiz, the team's scores are added up. At this point, determine which team scored the most points and which saboteur misled the team the best.

Variations

Easier: Tell the teams that they have a saboteur somewhere in their team.

Harder: Let the saboteurs see the questions and the correct answers the night before the game so they can plan.

70

Show Jumping

Learn definitions.
Encourage quick but accurate answers.

Equipment

- A glossary
- The show jumping course (see page 89)
- A stopwatch

Description

Pupils pair up; one pupil is the jumper whilst the other is the course official. The objective of the game is to get around the course as quickly as possible without incurring any faults or penalties.

Each fence represents a keyword (read aloud by the course official); to successfully jump the fence, the pupil must provide an accurate definition. The race official times how long it takes the pupil to complete the course and adds the penalty seconds to the pupil's time to obtain the final time. When the course is completed, the pupils exchange roles. At the end of the game, the winner is the jumper with the fastest time.

Faults and Penalties

- Knocking over a fence (providing an incorrect definition) earns a 20-second penalty.
- Refusing the fence (passing on a definition) earns a 40-second penalty.

Variations

Easier: Read the definition aloud, and the pupils have to provide the keyword.

Harder: Change some of the fences to questions.

Show Jumping Course

Tick the fence if jumped successfully	
Circle the fence if the fence is knocked over	
Cross the fence if the fence is refused	
Time finished	
Total time with faults included	

From G. Long, H. Grout, and S. Taylor, 2011, *101 Classroom Games* (Champaign, IL: Human Kinetics).

71

Snakes and Ladders

Make educated guesses or predictions.

Equipment

Two chairs

Description

Two pupils are selected to sit in the two chairs with their backs to the class. They are asked a question that requires them to guess or predict something (for instance, the height of Mt. Everest). Both pupils' answers are written on the board, and then the rest of the class has 10 seconds to stand behind the pupil whose answer they think is the closest to the actual answer. All those who stood behind the closest pupil earn 1 point. Select two more pupils and repeat the process with another question.

Every few questions, the teacher will throw in a snakes and ladders question. For these questions, standing behind the pupil with the closest answer earns 3 points (ladder) but standing behind the other pupil earns a deduction of 3 points (snake).

Variations

Easier: Provide a range the actual answer will be within.

Harder: Have four pupils and chairs so the pupils have more choices to make.

Snap

Practice answering examination questions.
Practice discussing answers and working as a team.

Equipment

- A set of question cards for each group
- A pack of playing cards for each group

Description

A group of four or so pupils plays a game of snap, with one difference: they can snap each time a suit is repeated rather than just a number. When a pupil successfully snaps, she then gets to draw a question card from the set and ask the other pupils the question on the card. The pupils can confer and then provide individual answers. The questioner earns 1 point for each incorrect answer. The game keeps going until all the questions have been asked.

Variations

Easier: Provide questions from different topics and allow the pupils to select their question.

Harder: The pupil who calls snap is asked the question and can earn points only if she can answer it.

Splat

Assess pupils' knowledge.
Encourage pupils to respond quickly to questions.

Equipment

- A classroom whiteboard
- Something that sticks to the whiteboard such as Blue-Tac
- A set of questions

Description

The whiteboard already has randomly written answers to the forth-coming questions (each answer has a circle drawn around it). The class is split into two teams, and a member of each team comes forward, a specified distance from the whiteboard, to answer a question from the teacher. Each pupil has a ball of adhesive in his hand. Pupils throw the adhesive at what they consider the correct answer. The correct answer is worth 100 points, which are divided among the number of teams who choose it (in this case, two). If both teams' representatives select the correct answer, they each earn 50 points. The next two pupils then come forward to answer the next question. The game can be played with more than two teams. Be sure to adjust the number of points awarded for the number of teams playing.

Variations

Easier: If both pupils miss the correct answer, allow points for the pupil whose ball sticks closest to the correct answer.

Harder: The winning team must throw their ball first, allowing the losing team to copy their answer. If both balls stick in the correct circle, both teams score 100 points.

Stand to Attention

Learn key concepts and definitions.
Improve recall and recognition.
Practice keyword recall.

Equipment

None

Description

Move all the desks and sit in a circle with the teacher sitting in the circle also. The aim of the game is to say words that are related to the main topic introduced by the teacher at the start of a game. Start by standing and stating a topic, such as circulatory system. Once you have sat down, the pupils have to stand, say a word or term related to the topic, and then sit down again. Each pupil has three lives. Pupils lose lives in one of three ways: if more than one pupil stands at the same time, if a pupil submits a wrong answer, or if a pupil is the last in the circle to answer.

Variations

Easier: Before each round, the teacher gives the pupils lists of possible content related to the topics to be covered. The teacher can modify the lists depending on the ability of the pupil. For instance, those who struggle could get a keyword and its definition, and the more able get the definition and must come up with the appropriate keyword.

Harder: The teacher can handicap the pupils by either changing the number of lives they have individually or by requiring the more able pupils to wait for 10 answers before standing.

Stand Up and Be Counted

Practice answering multiple-choice questions.
Develop confidence in their answers.

Equipment

A set of multiple-choice questions

Description

Pupils are put in teams of four, with members designated either A, B, C or D. Each team sits in alphabetical order whilst the teacher reads out a multiple-choice question. Once the question is read, the pupil designated the letter of the answer stands up. For example, if the answer is B, then pupil B should stand.

The following rules are employed throughout the game:

- No talking or conferring is allowed.
- If only the correct pupil stands, then the team scores 20 points.
- If the correct pupil stands up but so does one other member of his team, then 10 points are scored.
- If the correct pupil stands up but so do another two members of his team, then 5 points are scored.
- If all four pupils stand up, then 0 points are scored.
- If the pupil who represents the correct answer does not stand up, then the team scores 0 points.

Variations

Easier: Allow the pupils 10 seconds to confer and discuss the answer.

Harder: Do not award points unless only the correct pupil stands.

Steal a Brain

Recap key concepts.
Learn with different classmates.

Equipment

A set of questions

Description

The class is first organised into four to six teams. This game then works like a traditional quiz except for the scoring. Each individual pupil starts with 100 points; this will be the maximum number of points a pupil can score by the end of the game. If a team gets a question right, all pupils on that team maintain their scores, but if a team gets an answer wrong, all pupils in that team lose 5 points.

Before each question is asked, all teams that answered incorrectly can steal a pupil from a team that got the question right. (However, at least one pupil must be left remaining in each team at all times). Therefore, teams that have struggled get the option of improving their team, whilst those that have done well may have fewer team members for the next question.

Individual pupils must keep track of their own personal scores until the game ends. Pupils closest to 100 points by the end of the game are winners.

Variations

Easier: If a team has been wrong three questions in a row, allow them the option of freezing their score for the next question, but they are not allowed to earn another team member.

Harder: Allow a team to steal a classmate only if they are the sole team to get a question wrong.

Step Up to the Challenge

Assess pupils' knowledge.
Practice answering multiple-choice questions.

Equipment

- A set of multiple-choice questions
- A set of cards labelled A, B, C, D per student (see page 4)
- Sixteen cones

Description

All pupils stand in a line side by side. They may play as individuals or be put in teams. There are 10 cones in a column ahead of them and 5 behind them (see diagram). The finish line, and their goal, is the 10th cone in front of them.

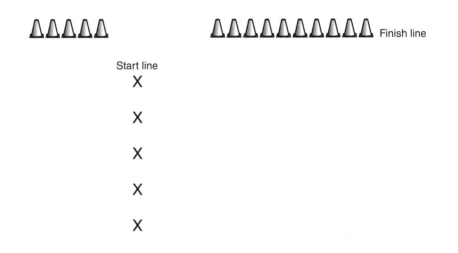

Read (or show on the screen) a multiple-choice question and provide the four possible answers. Any pupil who thinks she knows the answer raises her hand and steps forward to the cone in front of her. Any pupil who does not want to answer the question can pass and stay at her cone. Those who stepped forward show the card that corresponds with the answer. Those pupils who get the question right move forward one more cone (so at the start of the game, a pupil who answers correctly would end up on cone two). If those who stepped forward get the answer wrong, they must go back 2 cones (so at the start of the game they would now be on the cone behind the start cone). The winner is the first person (or team) to cross the finish line (past all 10 cones).

Variations

Easier: Pupils have two lives; if they get an answer wrong, they can play one of their lives and not move back.

Harder: Limit the pupils to two consecutive passes, so that they have to attempt some answers they may not be sure of.

Stop the Clock

Work on concept or topic recognition.
Improve understanding of links between topics.

Equipment

Method of displaying the score (whiteboard and board markers)

Description

You may have pupils play as individuals against each other or split the class into teams to have a whole class game.

Divide the class into two teams. This is a simple game where the quizmaster reads a description of a topic or a keyword. The quizmaster must describe the keyword without mentioning it. As soon as the quizmaster starts the description, he starts the clock (which will count down from 30 seconds), and each team may confer whilst the quizmaster reads the description. The quizmaster stops the description and pauses the clock when a team shouts, 'Stop the clock!' If that team answers correctly, they win the round. If they answer incorrectly, they are frozen out and cannot provide another answer (a full explanation follows), and the description continues until a correct answer is given.

'Stop the clock' relies on accurate timing by the quizmaster. The scoring is simple: The team or individual with the highest total time at the end of the game is the winner. Answering quickly allows the team or individual to guess the keyword or topic before the time runs down and the team which provides the correct answer score the number of seconds left on the clock. Care should be given not to give an incorrect answer and be frozen out. A team with a freeze-out (wrong answer) is penalized 15 seconds.

Variations

Easier: Only award a freeze-out for a team's second guess.

Harder: Try a no-call-out version of the game by giving each team a small whiteboard and pen or have them use pen and paper. Once a team thinks they have the answer, they write it down and raise it in the air.

Straws

Practice answering short-answer examination questions.

Equipment

- Three pieces of different-sized paper for each pupil
- Previous examination papers
- Music

Description

Each pupil has to write three different questions for their classmates to answer (they may use past examination papers for help). A three-mark question is written on the biggest piece of paper, a two-mark question is written on the medium-sized piece of paper, and a one-mark question is written on the smallest piece.

The pupils roll up the individual pieces of paper like straws and hold them upright in their hand so that another pupil cannot tell the values of the questions by the paper sizes. Begin playing music. The pupils walk around the room, and when the music stops, they meet another pupil. The pupils take turns selecting a straw and answering the selected question. The pupils keep count of their total score as they continue to meet other pupils.

Variations

Easier: Allow the pupils to read the previous examination papers before playing the game.

Harder: Allow the pupils to write some higher-value questions.

Strike a Deal

Learn key concepts.

Equipment

- Pupil A (contestant) worksheet (see page 102)
- Pupil A (contestant) worksheet (see page 103)
- Pupil B (quizmaster) worksheet (see page 104)
- A set of questions

Description

Based on the TV game show Strike a Deal, pupils work in pairs: One pupil is the contestant (pupil A) and the other pupil is the quizmaster (pupil B). The aim of the game is for the contestants to win as much money as possible without losing their three lives.

The quizmaster (pupil B) is given worksheet (page 104), and is told to keep the details of each box value a secret from the contestant (pupil A). The contestant has three lives; once he loses all three lives, he is out and wins no money.

The contestant chooses a box (for instance, number six) and tries to answer a question that is provided by the quizmaster. If the contestant answers incorrectly, he loses one life; if he answers correctly, he wins the value of the box (in this case, 50 dollars/pounds/euros). When the contestant wins some money he records this on his worksheet so that he knows what money is still out there. After three rounds of questions, the quizmaster totals the money won by the contestant and offers him 60 percent of that value of the prize money.

The contestant must consider how many lives he has left, how much money he has been offered, and then decide whether to bank the money offered by the quizmaster. If the contestant decides to bank the money, the game is completed, and this (60 percent of the total won) is the contestant's final score. If the contestant decides not to bank, he must try to answer three more questions correctly.

If the contestant progresses through the next three rounds (with at least one life still intact), the quizmaster adds up the prize money won and again offers the contestant 60% of this total. The contestant must again decide whether to bank or not bank. Once the contestant gets to the last three boxes, the quizmaster offers 60 percent of the prize money won after each question. The game is completed once the contestant banks the money offered, loses his three lives, or opens the final box.

Variations

Easier: Increase the number of lives the contestants can have. Provide multiple-choice questions for the contestant.

Harder: For each box, the contestant must answer two or more questions. Increase the number of boxes in the game.

Strike a Deal: Pupil A Worksheet

1	2	3
4	5	6
7	8	9
10	11	12

From G. Long, H. Grout, and S. Taylor, 2011, *101 Classroom Games* (Champaign, IL: Human Kinetics).

Strike a Deal: Pupil A Worksheet

Box value	Answered
$1	
$5	
$50	
$100	
$500	
$1000	
$5000	
$10,000	
$20,000	
$50,000	
$75,000	
$100,000	

From G. Long, H. Grout, and S. Taylor, 2011, *101 Classroom Games* (Champaign, IL: Human Kinetics).

Strike a Deal: Pupil B Worksheet

1 $1000	2 $5000	3 $1
4 $10,000	5 $100,000	6 $50
7 $20,000	8 $100	9 $500
10 $75,000	11 $50,000	12 $5

From G. Long, H. Grout, and S. Taylor, 2011, *101 Classroom Games* (Champaign, IL: Human Kinetics).

Super Bowl

Learn key concepts and definitions.
Practice recall and recognition.
Practice multiple-choice questions.
Recognise strengths and weaknesses in knowledge.

Equipment

- Photocopied football fields
- Question lists

Description

Split the class into small groups with the size depending on how many games you want going on at any one time. Teams compete against each other by asking questions based on topics of your choice. Each game will be refereed by a head referee who will also ensure that all the questions are legitimate. Each game will require an outline of an American football field. A good option is to photocopy onto A4 or A3 paper the image at this Web site: (http://static.howstuffworks.com/gif/football-diagram1.gif). An even better option is to use the front whiteboard or an interactive whiteboard for a Super Bowl event, playing one half of the class against the other.

Scoring

In American football, the ball-carrying team can make four attempts (downs) to move the ball 10 yards up the field towards the opponent's end zone. Each question, if answered fully and correctly, is worth 10 yards to the team in possession; however, if they answer incorrectly they may make three more attempts to answer correctly to make the 10 yards required to continue on to another question. If they are unable to provide a correct answer then possession is lost. All movements can be drawn on the paper or board, with each possession starting from the team's own goal line; thus each team must go the whole length of the field to score. Correct answers will advance the team in possession, gaining 10 yards each time. Once the team in possession reaches 10 yards from the end zone, they must choose between going for a touchdown or attempting a field goal. Touchdowns are worth 6 points whereas field goals are only worth 2. The touchdown questions should be harder to answer than the field goal questions, and neither should allow the team in possession to answer more than once. Possession is lost if the team fails to complete a 10-yard play or fails to score during an attempt for a touchdown or field goal. Possession immediately changes once points are scored.

Variations

Easier: Allow the referee to add penalties for infringements, such as inappropriate comments to the other team, causing a loss or gain of yardage. For example, insulting the other team could penalize the insulting team 10 yards or give 10 yards to the team that was insulted.

Harder: To make the game harder, separate the questions into 2-, 5-, 7-, and 10-yard questions (have the questions get harder as the yardage increases) and allow one question to gain the full 10 yards. Introduce special plays or teams, such as a punt, that occur under certain game conditions (for instance, if the team in possession struggles to reach their 10-yard mark, they may decide to kick possession away and get their opponents to start further downfield).

Surf's Up

Learn key concepts and definitions.
Practise recall and recognition.
Recognise strengths and weaknesses in knowledge.

Equipment

- Question lists
- Computer with Internet access

Description

To play, select a simple flash game from the Internet. Here we'll use a surfing game, but any game where points are awarded will work. Enter 'surfing flash game' into your Internet search engine and select a game for your pupils to play. Study the playing instructions before you set your pupils up to play.

Players

This game allows pupils to play as individuals or as a team.

- Singles: play 1v1
- Team knockout: each team selects a surfer to compete

Riding the Wave

Get the challengers to come towards the screen. Outline how to control the surfboard rider and how to score points. Each surfer has one minute to ride the wave and score as many potential points for his team as possible. Record the score at the end of each ride. The highest scoring surfer (or his team) gets to go first.

Scoring

Use multi-mark questions. Each surfer will be given the chance to score points relative to the top score from his ride. Announce the marks available for the first question and have both teams divide their scores by the number of marks possible. For instance, if surfer A scored 780 points, and surfer B scored 1100, and there were four marks available for the question, surfer A would be given 195 points for a correct answer and surfer B would be able to earn 275 points (780 divided by 4 equals 195). Once the question has been asked, each team has 1 minute to write down a suitable answer to try to earn maximum points.

Variations

Easier: Give bonus points for the highest-scoring move on the wave.

Harder: Get the teams to produce their own questions from past papers and mark schemes, and use them when playing.

Tenpin Bowling

Learn key concepts.
Practise providing a range of answers.

Equipment

Tenpin bowling scorecard (see page 110)

Description

The aim of this game is for pupils to provide quick-fire answers to a question or to think of key areas or words related to a topic. Pupils can work in groups of two or more. The more pupils in a group, the more questions or topics you need.

Pupil A is given a question, and she has 30 seconds to provide as many answers or keywords as possible for the question or topic (a minimum of 10 possible correct answers or keywords is required for each question or topic). For every correct answer or keyword, she knocks down a pin. If she gets 10 correct answers or keywords, she scores a strike. If pupil A has not achieved a strike, she then has 30 seconds to think before being given another 15 seconds in which to provide any more answers. If she is able to provide 10 correct answers in 2 attempts, she scores a spare.

The scoring system is the same as in an actual tenpin bowling game. When she scores a strike, the pupil is awarded 10 points, plus a bonus of whatever is scored with the next two questions. In this way, the points scored for the two balls after the strike are counted twice. See the following example.

- Question 1, attempt 1: 10 pins (strike)
- Question 2, attempt 1: 3 pins
- Question 2, attempt 2: 6 pins

The total score from these throws is:

- Question 1: 10 + (3 + 6) = 19
- Question 2: 3 + 6 = 9
- Total: 28

Variations

Easier: Allow 1 minute for the first attempt and 30 seconds for the second attempt or reduce the number of pins to 6.

Harder: Allow those pupils who understand tenpin bowling scoring to introduce doubles and turkeys.

Tenpin Bowling Scorecard

Name	1	2	3	4	5	6	7	8	Total

From G. Long, H. Grout, and S. Taylor, 2011, *101 Classroom Games* (Champaign, IL: Human Kinetics).

The Hat

Learn key concepts and definitions.

Equipment

- A set of keywords and associated definitions
- A hat

Description

Choose some keywords or concepts from the topic area being studied and put these on pieces of card; place these in the hat.

Read aloud a definition that matches one of the keywords in the hat. For example, you might read, 'The vessel that pumps oxygenated blood from the heart to the working muscles.'

Then, pull one of the keywords from the hat, read it aloud, and start a 10-second countdown. Pupils who think the keyword matches the definition stand up. During the 10-second countdown, pupils may stand and sit as they change their minds. If the keyword pulled is correct, pupils standing at the end of the countdown earn 10 points. If the keyword is wrong, those still standing are out of the game. Keywords are pulled and read until the correct keyword is pulled, and the 10-second countdown completed. At this point a new definition is read, and the game begins anew, with all pupils once again allowed to play and gain points.

Variations

Easier: Once a definition is read, all pupils write the correct term on a piece of paper and place it in the hat. One pupil draws one of the answers from the hat. If it is the correct answer, the class earns a point; if it is incorrect, the teacher earns a point.

Harder: Pupils can fool their classmates by standing up and down throughout the 10 seconds. But as soon as the teacher says stop, when 10 seconds are up, no more movement is allowed.

The Picture Board

Practise recall and interpretation.
Review key concepts and keywords.

Equipment

- Internet connection
- PowerPoint or similar presentation software
- Paper and pens

Description

Use an Internet search engine to find image galleries for pictures that represent items or concepts relating to your subject area. Make presentation slides of the pictures but distort them by cutting bits off, resizing them, or recolouring them so they are not so recognisable. Place these in a slide show and run it. Get each individual pupil to guess what each picture is or represents by writing three facts or pieces of information about the picture's concept or topic.

Once all pupils have had a chance to complete their answers, get them to review each other's work to determine their differences and similarities. Allow the pupils to modify their answers before they submit them for the final marking. Read the correct answers and get the pupils to total up their scores. Repeat the picture round when you cover the next topic or area.

Variations

Easier: Adjust the picture distortion so that it is easier to guess the picture's identity.

Harder: Eliminate the peer review section and mark the pupils' answers straight away.

Time Assault

Practise recognition and recall.
Practise thinking under pressure.

Equipment

- Question cards
- Stopwatch
- Whistle

Description

Form pairs of pupils and make one person in each pair the quizmaster (pupil A) and the other the challenger (pupil B). Push any furniture to the side and make sure that the pupils are suitably dressed for exercise. Time the group for one minute, using the whistle to start and stop the group.

At the whistle, all of the challengers begin running in place. Each quizmaster asks the first question as quickly as possible. Each challenger either answers or passes. After the whistle sounds again (at one minute), each quizmaster tells the teacher how many correct answers and how many passes to list on the board for pupil B. The players then swap roles: Pupil B asks the questions and pupil A answers. The countdown begins, and again the scores are tallied.

Repeat this for three rounds. With three sets of scores now on the board, total all the correct answers and subtract from the total the number of passes for teams A and B. The team with the greatest score at the end wins.

Variations

Easier: Start the running in place when the question has been read; this becomes think time for the challengers. They may stop again once they answer the question.

Harder: Give pupils a handicap system based on what you know about their performance under pressure.

Time Bombs

Recap or review previous work.
Encourage thinking under pressure.

Equipment

None

Description

The class stands in a circle facing inward. The teacher sets a timer for varying time lengths (it is great if the timer can sound like a ticking clock) and then names a topic area and a pupil's name. The selected pupil says a word associated with the topic and then names another pupil who repeats the process. Pupils earn a point for every accepted word, but the pupil whose turn it is when the time runs out is eliminated (he loses 2 points).

Variations

Easier: Divide the circle into four teams of different colours (use bibs), and each pupil must nominate someone from another team to answer.

Harder: Rather than just say one word, have the pupils provide more information or facts about their word.

Topic Lotto

Improve knowledge and understanding.
Evaluate an entire subject area.
Enhance recall and recognition of topic content.

Equipment

- Topic lotto boards
- Coloured cards or counters to fit the lotto board squares
- Exam questions and mark schemes

Description

This game can be played individually or in pairs. Give each player a lotto board. These can be made by drawing a 4 x 4 grid on a piece of paper or card. In each rectangle, place a topic title covering a section of the exam of interest. Make sure that each board has a similar selection of topic titles.

Select a question from the exam papers relevant to the topic titles on each board. Read the question to the class. Have the pupils write their answers in the appropriate box under the topic title. The teacher then reads the answer, and pupils with the correct answer may cover that section of their boards with a marker. If their answer is incorrect, they leave the space free to answer the next question under that topic title.

The first to cover all spaces of their board is the winner and shouts, 'Lotto!'

Variations

Easier: Use true and false or multiple-choice questions.

Harder: Modify the lotto boards by adding a larger number of the same topic squares so that they are encouraged to answer questions on their weaker topic areas.

Traffic Lights

Practise exam question responses.
Improve recall and interpretation.
Learn to self-assess.

Equipment

- Exam questions and mark schemes
- Green, yellow, and red sticky dots
- Paper for pupils' answers

Description

Set out three areas within the classroom that contain your three levels of exam questions. Place simple-answer questions in the green section, place the shorter-answer questions in the yellow section, and finally place the longer-answer (harder) questions in the red section.

Ask the pupils to visit the sections in any particular order, trying to answer as many questions as possible (on their paper) within a set time limit. The pupils check their answers against the mark scheme, which encourages honesty and a realistic assessment of their level of ability in that particular question area. If they answer correctly (fulfilling the mark scheme), they earn a dot of that section's colour.

When the time is up, ask each pupil to write a short action plan that identifies the topic areas they struggled with and outlines how they intend to develop that particular area. Make sure that they identify a time frame in which to complete the action.

Variations

Easier: Ask pupils to earn three green dots before they move on.

Harder: Prescribe the route that your pupils take around the traffic light system. You may decide that you wish your pupils to progress in an increasing difficulty fashion by limiting them to a green, yellow, red route. Alternatively you may wish to limit the number of easy questions attempted.

True or False?

Assess the knowledge and understanding of the class.

Equipment

- A true and false card for each pupil (see page 118)
- A set of true and false statements

Description

Each pupil is given a true and a false card. The teacher reads out a statement that may or may not be accurate. The pupils decide whether the statement is true or false and hold up the appropriate card. Pupils get 5 points for a correct answer. After every false statement, the pupils can earn bonus points if they can provide the true answer.

Variations

Easier: Pupils are allowed to ask the teacher one question before deciding on their answer.

Harder: Omit some words when reading the question for the first time. Pupils earn 10 points if they get the right answer on the first attempt, and 5 if they get it right on the second reading (when the full statement is provided).

True-or-False Card

That statement is true.

That statement is false.

From G. Long, H. Grout, and S. Taylor, 2011, *101 Classroom Games* (Champaign, IL: Human Kinetics).

Walkabout

Review key concepts and definitions.
Develop verbal explanations.

Equipment

- A set of A4 sized word cards
- Music

Description

The set of word cards (keywords and concepts from the previous lesson or topic) is spread face down on the classroom floor. The pupils walk around the room, and when they come face-to-face with another pupil, they each pick up a card. Both pupils take it in turns to describe or explain their word to each other; they then replace the card on the floor and move on. If neither pupil can accurately explain her word, she writes the word on a piece of paper. At the end of a set period of time, pupils read out the unexplained words they have recorded, and the teacher or another pupil explains that word to them.

Variations

Easier: Allow the pupils to work in pairs. You might also colour-code the back of the cards: green is an easy word while red is harder one.

Harder: Play musical chairs. Pupils stop to pick up a card when the music stops and must keep explaining the word until the music starts again.

What's the Question?

Understand key concepts and definitions.
Gain familiarity with examination answers.
Gain appreciation for the wording of examination questions.

Equipment

A set of examination answers

Description

The class is organised into teams. Show the teams a set of answers to a mystery examination question. The teams discuss the answers among their teammates and then provide a written question that they think relates to the answers. The teacher awards points to each team for the accuracy of their question before revealing the original question.

Variations

Easier: Show the class three possible questions; the teams have to choose the question that matches the answers shown.

Harder: Reveal the answers one by one and have the teams guess the question after seeing each answer. They then keep modifying the question until they have seen all the answers.

Which Way Is Best?

Encourage self-evaluation.
Have pupils evaluate their own learning styles.
Help pupils learn how to create personal learning material.

Equipment

- Paper, pens, and drawing equipment
- Whiteboard and board markers
- Computer access
- Topic resources: textbooks and so on

Description

Split the class into three groups. Ask the pupils to pair up within these groups, or alternatively, you decide which pairs will work most productively together and place them in these groups. At the start of the lesson, decide on a topic area that will be the focus for review. Bring a pair from each of the three teams to the front of the class and instruct them that they are going to teach their own teams the topic that you outlined. At the end of the teaching period (5 to 10 minutes), the class will have a short test on the topic. Each of the three paired teaching teams are given the same resources (magazines, Internet access, books) and will teach using one of the following review methods:

- Team 1: Diagrammatical (spider diagrams, flow charts, and so on)
- Team 2: Note-taking (lists, highlighting keywords, and so on)
- Team 3: Mind-mapping or analogy-learning (making stories, creating links)

After the teaching time is up, give a short test and record the scores. Now take another three pairs of teachers and give them another topic. Rotate the learning or memory method that the teams are exposed to.

Again, conduct a short test and record the scores. Finally, take another three pairs of teachers and assign the final topic. Rotate the learning or memory method again so that all three teams have used each of the methods. Complete the test and record again.

Total the correct answers from each of the three tests. The winning team is the team with the highest score. More importantly, your pupils have both taught and used three different methods of reviewing. Ask which method they found the most useful, and why they've come to that conclusion. This could have a positive impact on their review as a whole.

Variations

Easier: Allow the use of all three review methods in one lesson or alternatively, spread them out over three lessons.

Harder: Try a number of other review methods and get the pupils to teach and be taught using them to see if it benefits their final test scores. You can also consider getting those who prefer one method to have a group review and share resources.

Who Am I?

Expand knowledge and understanding.
Practise quick-fire starters and plenary sessions during review.
Improve recognition of topics under pressure (exam conditions).

Equipment

Paper and pens

Description

This game can be played as a whole class or in any number of smaller groups. Give each pupil five pieces of A5 paper to fold in half so that each can stand in a mountain shape on the desk. Have them label the pieces one through five, using large numbers. Using a keyword glossary, choose a keyword or definition and break it into five parts, with each part improving the ease of keyword recognition.

Ask the pupils to determine how many clues they think it will take them to identify the correct keyword; they should place that numbered paper before them. Once all pupils have placed their markers on their desks, start the description of the term, reading one part at a time. After the teacher has read the first part, any pupils with the number one on his desk must either make an attempt to answer or forfeit the chance. If he answers incorrectly or forfeits, he must tip his number marker over to indicate he is out and get 5 points. However if he answers correctly, he scores the number of points that was written on his marker. The pupil with the lowest score is the winner.

Variations

Easier: Encourage the pupils to select the lowest number of clues by increasing the number of points for the larger point markers. For instance, you might decide that if a pupil selects 5 clues twice in the game, it carries double weight, and he scores 10 points.

Harder: Play some random rounds in which pupils roll a die, and the number rolled determines when they must answer (however, a six means they can still choose the number of clues that they require).

Who Wants to Be a Smartie?

Learn key concepts and definitions.
Practise multiple-choice questions.

Equipment

- Candy or Monopoly money
- The quiz board (see page 125)
- A set of 'starter' questions
- A set of multiple-choice questions

Description

This game is based on the quizshow 'Who wants to be a millionaire.' Pupils work in pairs, one as the quizmaster and the other pupil as the contestant. The challenge for the contestant is to win as much candy (or money) as possible. To begin, the pupil is asked a 'starter' question to determine how many lifelines they may win. The 'starter' question has four answers (e.g., "Name 4 European capital cities."); lifelines are awarded depending on the number of correct answers the contestant supplies. The lifelines can be used for later questions.

- 1 correct answer: Ask a friend.
- 2 correct answers: 50/50 (where two of the possible answers are removed).
- 3 correct answers: Use the textbook for 1 minute.
- 4 correct answers: Ask the teacher.

The contestant works her way up the quiz board, answering as many questions as possible. Each question has four possible answers, and the contestant must choose the correct answer in order to progress. If the contestant does not know the correct answer, she can use a previously-earned lifeline, guess the answer, or decide to bank, thus keeping what she has currently won.

Once a contestant reaches the bank mark, that candy or money is safe. So, for instance, if the contestant answers the 32 Smarties question incorrectly, she will still win 12 smarties or points.

Variations

Easier: Provide only two possible answers rather than four.

Harder: The pupils design their own questions (with answers) to ask their partners.

Quiz Board for Who Wants to Be a Smartie?

32 Smarties	Question 8
24 Smarties	Question 7
16 Smarties	Question 6
BANK 12 Smarties	Question 5
8 Smarties	Question 4
BANK 4 Smarties	Question 3
2 Smarties	Question 2
1 Smartie	Question 1

Lifelines Used

Ask a friend

50/50 (two possible answers are removed)

Use the textbook for 1 minute

Ask the teacher

From G. Long, H. Grout, and S. Taylor, 2011, *101 Classroom Games* (Champaign, IL: Human Kinetics).

Winner

Reinforce key concepts and definitions.
Practise answering quickly and accurately.
Work on keyword review.

Equipment

- A set of questions
- Party noisemakers

Description

Pupils get together in groups of four to six. One is designated the quizmaster and each has a noisemaker in his mouth. The goal is for the pupils to be the first group to spell winner. Pupils stand in a circle while the quizmaster asks quick-fire questions. If a pupil knows the answer, he blows his noisemaker (which acts as a buzzer). If he answers correctly, he earns the letter W, and the group is on its way to spelling winner. If he gets the question wrong, he may nominate one of the other pupils to earn a letter.

Variations

Easier: Modify the game by giving different pupils different words to spell.

Harder: Change the rule so that an incorrect answer means that a pupil loses a letter.

Wise Words

Learn key concepts, and describe and expand them.
Develop communication skills.

Equipment

A set of keyword cards for each team (see template on page 128)

Description

This is a game for two teams. Teams A and B are both given a set of cards; each card has a keyword on it with three lines below the word. (See page 128.) On each card's lines, each team adds additional words related to the keyword at the top. For example, if the keyword was heart, the team may add blood, chamber, and aorta. After a set time, team A gives their cards to team B and vice versa. One team member then has to describe the keyword on his card for his team to guess. Teams earn 1 point for each keyword correctly guessed by a teammate as long as none of the following rules was broken:

- They cannot use any of the listed words.
- They are not allowed to mime.
- They are not allowed to use hand gestures.
- They are not allowed to say, 'It sounds like.'

Variations

Easier: Allow the pupils to use the listed words for fewer points (for instance, 2 points are earned for not using the listed words; 1 point is earned if they do use a listed word).

Harder: Limit the team to one guess per card. If the team passes or gets it wrong, the card is put to the back of the pack.

Wise Words Template

Keyword:
You cannot use any of the following words:
1.

2.

3.

Keyword:
You cannot use any of the following words:
1.

2.

3.

Keyword:
You cannot use any of the following words:
1.

2.

3.

Keyword:
You cannot use any of the following words:
1.

2.

3.

From G. Long, H. Grout, and S. Taylor, 2011, *101 Classroom Games* (Champaign, IL: Human Kinetics).

Withdrawal

Learn key concepts.

Equipment

26 coins for every two students

Description

Pupils play in pairs against each other. They place 20 coins in the middle of the table; each pupil keeps 3 coins. Toss a coin to decide who goes first.

Pupil A asks pupil B a question, and pupil B can choose to provide one, two, or three answers. For each correct answer, the pupil takes that number of coins out of the middle. If a pupil is unable to provide an answer, she places a coin back in the middle of the table. Pupils alternate asking questions. The pupil who picks up the most coins is the winner.

Variations

Easier: Every correct answer is worth two coins.

Harder: Increase the number of coins. Play the game in groups of four or more so players start to develop tactics.

Whiteboard Wonders

Reinforce key concepts and definitions.
Enhance recall and recognition.
Review keywords.

Equipment

- Large paper or a flip chart
- Whiteboard
- Large marker pens

Description

The aim of the game is to guess what a team member is trying to describe using drawings only. This is a great game that can be played in pairs or in large teams to get everyone involved.

One member of the team is given a keyword and has to get his teammate to guess what it is from the drawings he sketches on the paper or board. The artist has only 30 seconds in which to draw items from which the onlookers deduce what the keyword is. If the team cannot guess, the opposition team can attempt to guess. If they are correct, the points go to them.

Pass the pen and keywords to the other team to take a turn. Play to the best of five, and either change the keyword topic or challenge another team.

Variations

Easier: Allow each team to have three lives, allowing them to pass on a keyword in the list. This loses one life for the team.

Harder: Allow both teams to guess and shout out answers as the player attempts to draw the clues through pictures.

Word Grids

Learn keywords.
Encourage literacy within a particular topic.
Review and recap previous work.

Equipment

A word grid for each pupil, pair, or team (see page 132)

Description

Each pupil (or team) is given a copy of a word grid that the teacher has filled out. Write several categories or topics along the horizontal line of the grid (for example, the circulatory system, the respiratory system). The teacher randomly picks a letter from the alphabet, and the pupil (or team) has one minute to write words related to the topic that begin with that letter (for the example here, the team may come up with 'atrium' and 'alveoli' for the letter A). After the minute is up, the teacher selects another letter, and the process is repeated.

Variations

Easier: The teacher may predetermine the letters to be chosen rather than select them randomly.

Harder: Ask pupils to include more than one word for each category.

Word Grids Template

Letter	Topic 1:	Topic 2:	Topic 3:	Topic 4:	Topic 5:

From G. Long, H. Grout, and S. Taylor, 2011, 101 Classroom Games (Champaign, IL: Human Kinetics).

Word Rebounds

Learn key concepts.
Improve knowledge and understanding.
Work on keyword recall.
Practise performing under pressure (exam conditions).

Equipment

None

Description

Pupils work in groups of three. Provide each pupil with a different topic and give them five minutes to write as many keywords associated with that topic.

Pupil A—Topic 1

Pupil B—Topic 2

Pupil C—Topic 3

This game is played in three rounds. In the first game, pupil B plays pupil C, and pupil A is the judge. The judge starts the game by stating the name of their topic. Pupil B has five seconds to provide a keyword associated with that topic (the judge can ask for clarification if she feels that the word is not relevant). Once pupil B provides an answer, pupil C has five seconds to provide another answer. Pupil B provides a third, and the process continues until neither pupil can provide an answer in the time provided. The second game is pupil A versus pupil C, with pupil B as the judge. In the third game, pupil A plays pupil B, and Pupil C is the judge.

Variations

Easier: Extend the time to provide a word to 10 or 15 seconds. Allow pupils a time-out to write down some words that they may use if stuck.

Harder: Limit some pupils to words that begin with certain letters.

ABOUT THE AUTHORS

Gareth Long earned an MSc coaching degree from Loughborough University in the United Kingdom. He is a senior lecturer and programme leader in coaching and physical education at University College Plymouth of St. Mark and St. John in Plymouth, England. In leading a team of instructors in teaching theoretical physical education, Long became interested in using games to facilitate classroom learning. He is the editor of *Soccer IQ*, an online coaching resource. In his leisure time, he enjoys playing and coaching football (meaning soccer, of course!).

Harvey Grout is a senior lecturer in sport coaching at the University of Gloucestershire in Gloucestershire, England. He earned an MSc in physical and health exercise in sport psychology and previously taught physical education for six years. He has also served as a physical education tutor for the postgraduate certificate in education and is the founder of careers-in-sport.com. He enjoys playing cricket, football, and golf.

Stuart Taylor is a lecturer of coaching and physical education at University College Plymouth of St. Mark and St. John. He is currently completing his MSc in performance analysis at the University of Wales Institute Cardiff (UWIC). He earned his physical education teaching degree from Manchester Met, Alsager. Stuart was the head of key stage 5 physical education and sport at one of the UK's first sports colleges, where he developed an interest in engaging students through practical games in the classroom environment. Stuart is editor of *Sport IQ* online resources and is a national INSET presenter for examination physical education. In his spare time, he likes to surf, ski, and coach rugby.

You'll find other outstanding physical education resources at
www.HumanKinetics.com

In the U.S. call 1.800.747.4457
Australia 08 8372 0999
Canada. 1.800.465.7301
Europe . . . . .+44 (0) 113 255 5665
New Zealand . . . 0064 9 448 1207

HUMAN KINETICS
The Information Leader in Physical Activity
P.O. Box 507